LOOKING FOR MR. JEFFERSON

LOOKING FOR
MR. JEFFERSON
Clyde N. Wilson

SHOTWELL
COLUMBIA   SO. CAR.
EST. 2015
PUBLISHING

Produced in the Republic of South Carolina by

SHOTWELL PUBLISHING LLC

Post Office Box 2592

Columbia, So. Carolina 29202

www.ShotwellPublishing.com

Cover Design by Boo Jackson.

ISBN: 978-1-947660-96-0

FIRST EDITION

10 9 8 7 6 5 4 3 2 1

CONTENTS

LOOKING FOR MR. JEFFERSON

THE UNKNOWN JEFFERSON

JEFFERSONIANS

Jefferson and the Historians

A Lost American Legacy

*"A morsel of genuine history, a thing
so rare as to be always valuable."*

—Thomas Jefferson

Preface

I HAVE LONG THOUGHT OF JEFFERSON as the premier American Founder and statesman. This admiration began earlier than I can remember and has been a recurrent theme in my career as an historian. Jefferson has, of course, received multiple and contradictory interpretations and evaluations over the generations. Much of this attention has involved opinion rather than fact—Jefferson distorted as a symbol for purposes of the interpreter.

Jefferson has been the subject of quite a few of my articles, lectures, and book reviews. I like to think that I have gotten closer to the real Jefferson than most of those who have written about him and that my view of this great subject has some unique value. So, I have presumptuously collected for publication some of my writings on the subject. The comments were written over more than half a century. Most have been posted online although there is some new material here. There is some repetition, but restating neglected or forgotten facts does no harm. Some pieces were lectures for the Abbeville Institute and have retained that form.

And I still think that Jeffersonian democracy is the best kind of democracy if we could only find it again.

Clyde N. Wilson

Dutch Fork, South Carolina

2023

"The Marats, Dantons, Robespierres of Massachusetts are in the same pay, under the same orders, and making the same efforts to anarchise us, that their prototypes in France did there."

—Thomas Jefferson to the Marquis de LaFayette,
14 February, 1815

THE UNKNOWN JEFFERSON

1.

Looking For Mr. Jefferson

A CYNICAL BUT TRUE SAYING that sometimes passes around among historians is "He Who Controls the Present Controls the Past." Man is a symbolizing creature and political struggles can be as much over symbols as over tangible things. Those who hold power and those who seek power want to associate themselves with favourable symbols from their society's past. It gives them an air of tradition and legitimacy. Those who hold political, cultural, educational, and media power obviously have an advantage in this game. Or sometimes the game is associating rivals with negative symbols. Who does not want to be likened to Lincoln and to stick their opponents with Hitler?

Needless to say, none of this has much to do with historical accuracy, which even at its best is an elusive and to some degree an unavoidably subjective thing. Thomas Jefferson was for a long time one of the most potent references in American discourse. I can think of nobody else who has had this role so powerfully as both a negative and a positive symbol. Jefferson's name is still significant, as we witness the relentless efforts of the present regime, which fears the real Jefferson, to destroy him as a favourable image. But I am sorry to report to this gathering that Mr. Jefferson is no longer as important as he once was, nor does he have the meaning for most Americans that he once had. We live in an age of reverence for Franklin D. Roosevelt, John F. Kennedy, and Martin Luther King, and in a time in which eighteenth and nineteenth century America is as remote to most citizens as ancient Persia or China.

Despite the fact that he is one of the most heavily documented figures of his time, we have a hard task in locating the real Jefferson because he has been a symbol so used and manipulated and distorted by successive generations of power seekers. One thing we ought to make clear from the start: Thomas Jefferson was not a guru giving the holy word to his disciples, though he has been made to play that role. He certainly never considered himself to be such and such a concept was alien to American discourse in his time and well after. He did not get the Declaration of Independence from Heaven and single-handedly promulgate it to initiate a world revolution of liberty and equality. He was the draftsmen who was charged with making a statement that would justify the rightfulness of the thirteen colonies having become thirteen free and independent States. As a public man, Mr. Jefferson was always a representative of the people, not a prophet.

We should remember that Jefferson's idea of his public role was an illustration of republican ethics. A good republican who held office and returned to the people to live quietly under the laws he had made. He did not hector those who succeeded him in the responsibilities of office. Mr. Jefferson departed Washington and never thereafter left the soil of Virginia. For the rest of his life he did not make speeches, give interviews for publication, or hold press conferences. He did privately answer queries on public affairs from people that he trusted.

Mr. Jefferson lived so long and wrote so much to so many people that it is easy to cherry pick words to support almost any agenda. Jefferson was a cosmopolitan intellectual with a worldwide reputation, recognized in the Old World and the New as a wise and good man. But as an American public man he was the Virginian statesmen who saved the Constitution from the centralizing and rent-seeking agenda of the Federalists and preserved it as had been intended in its ratification. His was the name most often revered and invoked as the symbol of the values of the agrarian majority of Americans outside the sphere of New England influence. It is worthwhile to distinguish the intellectual speculations of a great mind from the solid positions of the public man.

He did not become a guru until well into the 19th century, when "All Men are Created Equal" became a mystical and emotional invocation in a time that was more romantic and less clear-minded than that of the American Founders. The phrase was used to great effect by Abraham Lincoln and by Karl Marx, who in support of Lincoln's war, proclaimed the American Declaration to be blood kin to the French Declaration of the Rights of Man. Anyone who will read Jefferson's *A Summary View of the Rights of British America*, written just two years before the Declaration, will see that he wrote more in the spirit of Magna Carta than that of the French Revolution. The Democratic party of Jefferson's time and several generations thereafter did not deck out its conventions and newspapers with banners reading "All Men are Created Equal." The banners read: "The Principles of '98!" The Kentucky Resolutions affirming that sovereign authority rested in the people acting through their States.

Mr. Jefferson had ideals and until his later years was an optimist, but he was never an ideologue or an abstractionist. He believed that, with enlightenment, humanity could make progress. I do not think he believed in Progress with a capital "P" that was some inevitable law of history, as reformers and revolutionaries have postulated. He thought that Americans had a unique opportunity to preserve free institutions if they were wise and virtuous. He did not believe that Americans were a Chosen People with a divine mission to spread freedom to all mankind. That idea was invented by the New Englanders who hated him and who he despised.

During the hectic revolutionary 1790s, Jefferson lived peacefully among his many slaves, while John Adams was fortifying his house in fear that the American mob would imitate their French peers. President Adams insisted on being addressed as "Your Excellency" and riding in a fancy carriage. Jefferson walked to his inauguration, introduced relaxed manners into White House social occasions, and sent his annual message in writing to Congress rather than delivering it to the assembled congressmen like the monarch from the throne. It was the difference between a real aristocrat and a wannabe aristocrat.

We can never understand Mr. Jefferson's role in American history without recognizing the hatred he aroused in the New England intelligentsia and the distaste with which he regarded them. We know that the New England clergy denounced him from the pulpit in 1800 and later as a Jacobin infidel who would set up the guillotine and share out the women.

Listen to the young Connecticut poet William Cullen Bryant, addressing Jefferson in response to the Louisiana Purchase:

> Go wretch, resign thy presidential chair,
>
> Disclose thy secret measures, foul or fair.
>
> Go, search with curious eyes for horned frogs
>
> 'Mid the wild wastes of Louisiana bogs;
>
> Or, where the Ohio rolls his turgid stream
>
> Dig for huge bones, thy glory and thy theme.

The good young Yankee evidently regarded Jefferson's interest in science as a sign of atheism and could only see Jefferson's provision of vast lands for future generations of Americans as an evil invitation to the disorder that was bound to come when people escaped from New England dominance to the freedom of the wilderness.

Jefferson returned the compliment. He writes to John Taylor in 1798:

> It is true that we are completely under the saddle of Massachusetts and Connecticut, and that they ride us very hard, cruelly insulting our feelings, as well as exhausting our strength and substance.

He further remarked that the Yankees were marked with such a "perversity of character" that they would always be divided from other Americans. In his letter to Washington justifying his departure from the administration, he writes that every act of the new government had been designed to profit the North at the expense of the South. His stand could have been made by any Confederate of 1861. His comments on "perversity of character" might apply equally well to today's celebrity intelligentsia who are busy blackening his name.

On one occasion during his retirement, Mr. Jefferson was visited at Monticello by Noah Webster of Connecticut. Webster's *American Dictionary* was really a New England dictionary. In the introduction, Webster explained that New Englanders spoke the best and purest English of any people in the world and he indulged in raptures about the superior wisdom and virtues of his region. Jefferson described Webster to Madison as "a mere pedagogue of very limited understanding and very strong prejudices and party passions."

I have always thought that Jefferson's advocacy of the separation of church and state was in part inspired by his distaste for the political power of the Yankee clergy. Remember, the famous letter about "the wall of separation" was addressed to a group of Baptists in Connecticut, who were independent of that State's established Puritan church. One can still find die-hard Calvinists who denounce Jefferson as an atheist. For some reason they never mention that John Adams became a Unitarian.

Through the 19th century Jefferson remained a very popular symbol among the people and occasionally among writers, but New Englanders tended to dominate the print culture. This was a very calculated and largely successful program of the New England elite to make up for their political eclipse by capturing American discourse and symbols. Jefferson noticed this. He mentions, for instance, that several writers had given credit to Massachusetts for a step toward independence that belonged to Virginia. The Hemmings charge gained traction because New Englanders routinely and relentlessly charged that all Southern men acted that way. You see, New Englanders were models of sturdy Christian character while Southerners were lazy, incompetent, and of depraved morals. The literature spreading this viewpoint is massive from the 1790s up until the Civil War and even after.

In the early 20th century the *American Nation* series was published as a definitive multi-volume history of America for libraries and upper middle-class parlors. The volume on the Jefferson era was given to the Harvard historian Edward Channing. He describes Jefferson as "shambling" and his administration as incompetent. In 1905 New Englanders are still manly and dignified achievers and Southerners are still sloppy and contemptible.

Through the 19th century, and especially after the war to "preserve the Union," the respectable American symbolic founder in published literature, after Washington, was Hamilton; Jefferson was a lesser and somewhat dubious figure. But as time went on he could not avoid being nationalised to some degree. Teddy Roosevelt was able to invoke the Louisiana Purchase and the Monroe Doctrine as Jeffersonian precedents for imperialism. In my invariably humble opinion, Mr. Jefferson would not be pleased to become an icon on Mount Rushmore along with the blood and iron nationalists Lincoln and Roosevelt. His vision of peopling the North American continent with American farmers is something very different from Northern capitalists using the armed forces to seize Cuba and the Philippines.

If we had time it would be interesting to examine the subtle distortions of Jefferson's image that were promulgated by the Massachusetts historians George Bancroft and Henry Adams. But I want to turn to the restoration of Jefferson as a favourable symbol in the first half of the 20th century by thinkers and writers who might be called progressives or liberals. Charles Beard published his *Economic Origins of Jeffersonian Democracy* in 1915, and ten years later Claude G. Bowers produced *Thomas Jefferson and Alexander Hamilton: The Struggle for American Democracy.* They were joined by many others invoking Jefferson positively. Those who were unhappy with the domination of the American government by crony capitalism discovered that the Jeffersonians had opposed and foreseen such a sad state of affairs. The Jefferson Memorial was built in Washington by New Dealers and John Taylor of Caroline was revived as a great thinker and prophet.

We should be grateful for this wave of positive Jeffersonianism because it allowed opportunity and scope for Dumas Malone's masterwork. Yet this favourable image of Jefferson involved distortions that were almost as bad as the old Federalist ones. I doubt that Mr. Jefferson would have cared much for the centralizing policies of the New Deal. New Dealers engaged in incredible acrobatic feats of tortured interpretation to make Jefferson appear to be one of them.

The fight over the Jefferson symbol in recent years, I submit, has largely been a sham battle. On one side are those who want to preserve the inaccurate but comforting image of Jefferson as the 20th century liberal. On the other side are those liberals who have discovered the obvious fact that he is not one of them and therefore should be banished forever into the Outer Darkness.

No wonder Jefferson arouses a negative reaction among today's prevailing intelligentsia. It is impossible to imagine an American society that is more un-Jeffersonian than the regime we live under today.

Jefferson abhorred entangling alliances and hoped to preserve the great gulf between the New World and the Old. The U.S. today has a military presence in over a hundred places around the globe.

Jefferson envisioned a continent filled with the descendants of Americans, with a few Europeans with valuable skills invited in. Today the descendants of the original Americans are an ever diminishing minority in an international unmelting pot.

Jefferson's educational system was designed to nurture natural aristocrats who might be born into the unprivileged ranks of society, so that their talents and virtues would not be lost to the commonwealth. Instead, America early adopted the Massachusetts/Prussian system of public education designed to cultivate mass conformity and obedience.

Jefferson believed in the freedom of the mind to seek the truth and did not fear any genuine truth. We live in a society virtually without any real debate, dominated by Cultural Marxism.

Jefferson abhorred judicial oligarchy that thwarted the will of the people. Today the Supreme Court, not the people of the States, has sovereign power.

Jefferson feared banks and paper money. Our society is now dominated by banks that are Too Big to Jail.

Jefferson hated public debt. It placed a tax burden on the productive in order to profit the privileged unproductive, John Taylor's "paper aristocracy." Not only that, Jefferson's constant theme throughout his life was that "the earth belongs to the living." For the current generation to bind future generations down with debt was deeply immoral and anti-democratic. What would he make of our catastrophic national debt? That much of it is owed to foreigners, Mr. Jefferson would undoubtedly label as treasonable.

The reason that people today have such trouble dealing with Jefferson and slavery is that when they think of slavery they think of something different than what Jefferson saw. We look at slavery through a nationalist and abolitionist lens that Jefferson did not have before his eyes when he regarded the subject. Jefferson lived all his life in a system of domestic, household slavery that had been a way of life for generations. He was on record about the undesirability of slavery and had done what he could to encourage its end. Like most thoughtful Southerners he regarded it as an unfortunate thing, but a thing so interwoven with society that nobody knew what to do about it—what he meant by "holding a tiger by the tail." Lincoln himself said in 1860 he would not know what to do even with plenipotentiary power.

Perhaps we can understand Jefferson's conception of slavery by quoting John Adams, who is falsely portrayed in television epics as an abolitionist. Here is Adams speaking on the Constitutional provisions regarding slavery. He thought that debate on slavery was a matter of words, not realities:

> ...that in some countries the laboring poor were called freemen, in others they were called slaves; but that the difference as to the state was imaginary only.... That the condition of the laboring poor in most countries, that of the fishermen particularly in the Northern States, is as abject as that of slaves.

Writing sympathetically to Jefferson at the time of the Missouri controversy. Adams remarked that he was entirely willing to leave the question of slavery to Southern men.

When you say "slavery" today people think of the blighted and barbaric South that was pictured by the abolition movement from the 1830s onward. The abolitionists were vituperative, accusatory, called on unconstitutional federal power, and were marked by an almost religious fanaticism. They had no constructive solutions regarding the life of Southern people, black or white. They were a product of the perverse Massachusetts and Connecticut character which Jefferson had always abhorred. For Jefferson slavery was something to be dealt with by Virginia in the light of reason. Like every other Southerner, Jefferson, had he been there, would have found abolitionism to be an irresponsible, disingenuous, slanderous, dangerous, and repugnant attempt to dictate to Virginia by people who would feel none of the consequences of their fury.

Any inconsistency or hypocrisy in regard to the issue is not in Jefferson, but in the eye of the beholder.

To understand this we need only look at Jefferson's response to the Missouri controversy—"the fire-bell in the night." Jefferson had of course fathered the prohibition of slavery in the Northwest Territory. But Missouri was not a territory but a State in which a sovereign people had incorporated themselves. Their constitution and domestic institutions were not to be overruled by the federal government. Furthermore, unlike the 1780s, the foreign slave trade was closed and there was not the likelihood of many more Africans being imported. In his letters to Lafayette and to John Holmes, it is clear that what alarmed Jefferson and filled him with despair about the American future was not the persistence of slavery but the fact that Northerners had gratuitously and with bad motives drawn an ineffable sectional line. The campaign for territorial restriction of slavery really had nothing to do with the institution but represented a power grab by the Northern interests who had been eclipsed in his revolution of 1800.

One of the most egregiously dishonest symbolizations in American history took place when the party proclaiming "free soil" after the Kansas-Nebraska acts gave itself the Jeffersonian name Republican. That party was based in the regions that had always been most anti-Jeffersonian. It had a mercantilist program that was the polar opposite of a Jeffersonian political economy. Further, the demand to exclude slavery from the territories came from a very different perspective than Jefferson's. When Jefferson looked westward he saw succeeding generations of Americans creating new self-governing commonwealths. The new Republican defenders of "the Union" saw something very different when they looked in that direction. They saw natural resources to be exploited, new markets to be developed behind a tariff wall that diverted wealth to favoured interests, more political offices to be filled by their party, more immigrants to be lured, which would keep down the wages of native labour and enhance the value of the lands to be given to corporations by the government. In their plans, black people, slave or free, were eternally excluded.

And for the crowning hypocrisy, the campaign against the "extension of slavery" violated completely Jefferson's only hope for emancipation. As he observed, the movement of slaves from one place to another did not create any new slaves, and the dispersion of the rapidly increasing African population was the best hope for amelioration and eventual freedom.

Jefferson was a patriot. He was not a nationalist advocate of "one nation indivisible." During and after his time, nationalism was becoming a dominant force in the Western world, including the plural States United. Nationalism meant a territory politically and economically controlled by a central state and an emotional attachment to that state. For Jefferson one could be an American patriot without requiring total and unreserved obedience to the central government or believing that the people were spiritually inseparable from that government.

American nationalists glory in imagining Jefferson, having consummated the Louisiana Purchase, sitting in the presidential mansion celebrating the growing power and glory of the mighty new nation, the United States of America. This picture is an invention of the imperialist impulse of the late 19th century. At the time Jefferson writes to a close associate:

> The future inhabitants of the Atlantic and Mississippi States will be our sons. We leave them in distinct but bordering establishments. We think we see their happiness in their Union, and we wish it. Events may prove otherwise; and if they see their interest in separation, why should we take side with our Atlantic rather than our Mississippi descendants? It

is the elder and the younger son differing. God bless them both, and keep them in union, if it be for their good, but separate them, if it be better.

A letter to the English savant Joseph Priestly, January 29, 1804, expresses the same sentiments. After expressing relief that the worrisome problem of the Napoleonic empire on the Mississippi has been solved, Jefferson writes:

> The denouement has been very happy; and I confess if I look to this duplication for the extending a government so free and economical as ours, as a great achievement to the mass of happiness that is to ensue. Whether we remain in one confederacy, or form into Atlantic and Mississippi confederacies, I believe not very important to the happiness of either part. Those of the western confederacy will be as much our children and descendants as those of the eastern....

The Union was not sacred and eternal. It was an arrangement that could be changed. What was important was the principle of self-government.

Perhaps the most egregious distortion perpetrated by the New Deal Jeffersonians was the dismissal of State rights—which indeed for Jefferson was not State rights but State sovereignty. According to them, State rights were not really important to Jefferson and Madison. They just resorted to a handy device for defending dissenters. This was no longer relevant because good liberals were now defending dissenters in the courts.

No honest person who reads the plain language of the Kentucky Resolutions and the relevant passage in the first inaugural can possibly believe this nonsense. State rights and American liberty were inseparable in Jefferson's mind—always. This idea he repeated again and again and again to the end of his life. And when Jefferson suggested the usefulness of a little rebellion now and then, what he had in mind was the people rising to curtail the usurpations of rulers and return the government to its original limited powers. Unlike those who later celebrated him as a hero of dissent, he did not advocate overthrowing society in favour of some new plan to be implemented by a powerful government.

Mr. Jefferson spent his last Christmas Eve in this earthly realm drafting a document that was designed to initiate Virginia nullification of the internal improvements legislation of the J. Q. Adams administration. This was less than three years before John C. Calhoun drafted the plan for South Carolina to nullify the protective tariff. Jefferson made the same points that Calhoun was to make: the laws were unconstitutional and exploitive of the South; the self-interested majority responsible for them was blind to all pleas for the redress of grievances. Therefore, the proper remedy was the interposition of state sovereignty.

During the same Christmas season of 1825, discussing his proposal for nullification, Mr. Jefferson writes this to William Branch Giles:

> We should separate from our companions only when the sole alternatives left, are the dissolution of the Union with them, or submission to a government without limits to its power. Between the two evils, when we must make a choice, there can be no hesitation.

There is no doubt that had Jefferson been around in 1861 he would have been, like Robert E. Lee and the families of all the great Virginia Founders, a reluctant secessionist but a firm Confederate in resistance to invaders who, like their forebears of 1798, were insulting the feelings and exhausting the substance of the Southern people.

2.

Jefferson and the Declaration

SEVERAL GENERATIONS AFTER HIS LIFETIME, Thomas Jefferson became best known, as he still is, for these words: "All men are created equal, and they are endowed by their Creator with certain unalienable rights, among which are Life, Liberty, and the Pursuit of Happiness."

Here is an important lesson in understanding American history. The American Founders tend to be treated as demigods who handed down the Declaration of Independence and the Constitution as universal, eternal, and sacred bequests to all mankind. This makes the words of the Founders both mystical and highly manipulable. When Jefferson wrote this famous passage, he was not a guru who was passing out divine wisdom designed to revolutionise the world. And he was certainly not launching a crusade in favour of equality. Such a way of looking at the Declaration is mystification perpetrated by people with an agenda. Jefferson believed in reason and despised vague, reverential thinking, which he knew had most often been used throughout history to cover up oppression. As he himself said, the American Founders were a good bunch of men who enjoyed a unique opportunity, but they were men, not gods or prophets, and their work was subject to examination by other men and later generations in the light of reason. John C. Calhoun and the

15

other spokesmen of the Old South, by the way, held the same philosophical and historical view, contrary to the false legalistic description of their Constitutional thought which has become standard.

The Declaration was not Jefferson's unique wisdom. He was only the draftsman of a document by which the Continental Congress explained to the people of the civilised world why the thirteen colonies were now independent States jointly fighting a defensive war against the British government. Neither he nor the Continental Congress which adopted his draft, after some revisions, had or presumed to have the authority or the intent to launch a campaign to spread the principles they cited to the rest of the universe.

"Rights" was already a familiar term of use in the English speaking world, and it fit into a traditional constitutional framework, as the use of the legal term "unalienable" suggests. The "Pursuit of Happiness" undoubtedly embraced the sanctity of private property, however unequal. That the Creator is the source of rights brings in Christian natural law. The Declaration is mostly a statement of complaints that justify resistance to a bad king. It is obviously in the tradition of Magna Carta and the English Glorious Revolution of 1688. There is nothing revolutionary about it in the modern sense of the term.

"When in the course of human events, it becomes necessary for one people to dissolve the political bands which have connected them with another...." The necessity has occurred. The thirteen colonies have a long history as self-governing societies, a condition which is now threatened. The occasion calls for a statement of rights violated, in the good old English tradition. Therefore "these United Colonies are, and of Right ought to be *Free and Independent States.*" There you have it: the sovereignty and self-government of existing free societies. Of course, as is always the case in human events, the declaration still had to be made good by the bayonet wielded by free men.

Mr. Jefferson was the drafter of a declaratory document to be adopted, or not, by the thirteen sovereigns. He was not Moses releasing a prophecy. Contrary to befuddled scholars, he did not get his fillip about Equality from reading French books. It came from his belief in the self-governing equality of Americans' primitive Anglo-Saxon ancestors before they succumbed to Norman centralism. "All men are created equal" meant that a Briton on this side of the water is just as damn good as a Briton on the other side, a second son is just as good as a first-born, and that no man is entitled, as the author said on another occasion, by birth "to ride booted and spurred over his fellows." Aristocrats were to be identified, as he said on yet another occasion, not by birth but by talents and services.

Every thoughtful American of the 19th century worried, and many said, that the unfortunate bit of language about equality was a cannon that might break loose on the deck and destroy everything in its path. Something had happened: the French Revolution, which endowed the minds of a large part of Western man with a vision of the Rights of Man bestowed by a centralized, self-justifying state. Equality had become an "armed doctrine" for the overthrow of society.

On this side of the water, there were several effects. The disintegration of New England Puritanism spawned utopian and blasphemous Transcendentalism and various enthusiastic religious cults. The thrust of these phenomena was to create a popular ideology which confused together God's plan for the Universe and the New Man's destiny of perfection with America's destiny as the trailblazer for mankind, or rather the New England version of America. (In an 1844 public letter to American leaders, Joe Smith, Connecticut born leader of the Mormons, called upon the Declaration's alleged Rights of Man as justifying the federal government's authority to overrule the states on behalf of his beleaguered sect.)

The second thing that occurred in the United States was another consequence of the French Revolution. Among the Germans the Revolution left a bastard offspring: an ideology even more abstract, ruthless, and state worshiping than the original. The human debris of the failed European Revolutions of 1848 poured into the free confederacy in America, which they assumed, mistakenly, was the embodiment of their version of the Rights of Man. It is easy to demonstrate that demographically, these Puritans and Forty-Eighters, along with ruthless economic exploiters, twisted politics out of its accustomed paths in the Midwest and made possible Abraham Lincoln's elevation to the Presidency by a 40 percent vote.

In the Gettysburg Address, Lincoln read the "armed doctrine" back into the Declaration. He claimed that it had "brought forth a new nation dedicated to the proposition that all men are created equal." He lied. The Declaration brought forth no new nation except in a vague and wishful sense. It announced that the thirteen colonies were rightfully free and independent States. The primary proposition of the Declaration is not equality.

Lincoln at Gettysburg was, of course, in the very act of egregiously violating the Declaration and the central proposition of the American Founders, the consent of the governed. In the same year that Lincoln spoke, Karl Marx wrote a manifesto in support of Lincoln. According to Marx, Lincoln was suppressing an evil rebellion of slaveholders that had sprung up in the "one great democratic republic whence the first Declaration of the Rights of Man was issued." Marx cared even less about the American founding than did Lincoln, but together they merged the American War of Independence and the French Revolution into one terrible armed doctrine justifying wars of domination. Thus Jefferson and the Founders have been routinely enlisted under a false banner and presented to the world as what they never were or wanted to be.

We begin to understand what Jefferson meant by equality when we read him many times in slightly different words avowing that "no men are born to ride booted and spurred on the backs of others." Americans were against the hereditary privilege that dominated old world societies.

The Declaration is put in context by Jefferson's pamphlet, *A Summary View of the Rights of British America.* This was written just two years before the Declaration, was his first significant public document, and was what gained him name recognition in the colonies. In his *Summary View,* Jefferson chastises the King for not recognising that Americans were and always had been free men consenting to their government. Their Anglo-Saxon ancestors as free men had chosen to migrate from northern Europe and created Britain. Then they migrated to the New World. Anglo-Saxons had not come to America as employees, wards, or servants of government. They had established commonwealths on their own initiative and at the risk of their own lives, limbs, and property. The British government had no standing in its present attempts to reduce Americans to subjects of a distant government. Although Jefferson was a good historian, we might quibble a bit about this history, which for one thing, overlooks the Norman conquest. But my point is the context in which he viewed equality.

If we need further insight into the matter of "all men are created equal," look at Jefferson's post-presidential philosophical dialogue with John Adams on government. Jefferson writes:

> ...there is a natural aristocracy among men. The grounds of this are virtue and talents.... There is also an artificial aristocracy, founded on wealth and birth, without either virtue or talents....The natural aristocracy I consider as the most precious gift of nature, for the instruction, the trusts, and government of society....May we not even say, that

that form of government is the best, which provides the most effectually for a pure selection of these natural *aristoi* into the offices of government.

Lincoln at Gettysburg declared that the Declaration had not made free and independent states, but a "nation." And specifically, a nation dedicated to the proposition of equality, presumably justifying its pursuit by *any means*. The bigger battalions made the reinterpretation stick. Contrary to what has countless times been said since, Lincoln was not proclaiming the equality of African-Americans, which was never a sincere goal and soon forgotten. He was proclaiming that the French Revolution had replaced the American Founding and would govern in the future. Anyone who will look honestly at the Union war will see that, aside from a few pretty speeches, it was justified in terms of blood and iron nationalism—an indestructible government.

Gone was the central idea of 1776, *consent*—that government required consent of the people governed. Consent could be given only once, and then was forever binding, not the recurrent process portrayed in the Declaration. The people were no longer the center, the government was. The plural United States were now an artificial singular. "American" which had meant the fellow feeling of related peoples now meant merely obedience to the same government.

A brave people's assertion of self-government has been turned into a maudlin search for an impossible Equality, in a non consensual, destroying society.

3.

A LITTLE REBELLION

SCANDALOUSLY, THOMAS JEFFERSON ONCE WROTE to James Madison, "I hold it that a little rebellion now and then is a good thing and is as necessary in the political world as storms in the physical." In the same year, 1787, in regard to what is known as Shays' Rebellion, he wrote another friend, "God forbid that we should ever be 20 years without such a rebellion." A lack of rebelliousness among the people would demonstrate "a lethargy, the forerunner of death to the public liberty...And what country can preserve its liberties if its rulers are not warned from time to time, that this people preserve the spirit of resistance?"

The "rebellion" in Massachusetts had alarmed many, especially the masters of that commonwealth, who were imbued with a Puritan longing for regulated behavior and saw the tax revolt of Capt. Daniel Shays and his farmers as a threat to their control. In Jefferson's perspective, the "rebels" were merely adhering to good American practice. What, indeed, had the recent War of Independence amounted to but resistance to heavy-handed government? And such rebellions against unsatisfactory government officials and policies had been a regular occurrence during the long colonial history of the Americans, especially in the Southern colonies.

Persistent misrepresentation of Jefferson's words here and elsewhere by later generations has obscured what he meant. A dangerous radical? A chronic upsetter of social order? No. Jefferson does not call for an overturn of society and its reconstruction according to some abstract plan. Think of the root meaning of the term revolution. Jefferson, in fact, is mostly satisfied with his society (Virginia), although he is interested in a few small reforms that might broaden its base. So are his followers satisfied with their portions of America. That is why they support him. Despite the hysterical and sometimes insincere denunciations of the New England clergy, the Virginia planter is no Jacobin. As he sees things, any government, with the passage of time and the accretion of abuses and bad precedents, becomes corrupted. It needs to be REVOLVED back to its original principles.

This is not a radical program but a deeply reactionary one. What Jefferson fundamentally wants to tell us is that the people should never fear the government, but the government should always fear the people. This is not the battle cry of a movement with a radical agenda. President Jefferson comes to the White House with no agenda except to preserve the joint independence of the States United and their separate rights as "the best bulwark of our liberties." To carry out this agenda requires a rollback of the economic and judicial corruptions introduced by the Hamilton/ Adams innovators.

For the Jeffersonian democrats, Americans were fortunate to enjoy widespread property ownership, with a large body of independent citizens, and to be free of the class hegemony and conflict of the Old World, thankfully an ocean away. There is no French or Russian revolutionary fantasy here. The government is not to be used as a sledgehammer to destroy and rebuild society. In this way of thinking, the greatest enemy of society and of individual liberty is government itself. The tendency of power is everywhere and forever toward concentration. As a popular Jeffersonian saying has it, "Power is always stealing from the many to the few."

It is this basic orientation that separates Jeffersonian democrats from "conservatives" of Jefferson's own time and later. It explains the curious phenomenon that throughout American history the people have been "conservative," and revolutionary changes have always come from the top down.

My point is illuminated by the argument between John Adams in his *A Defense of the Constitutions of the United States* and John Taylor of Caroline, the systematic philosopher of Jeffersonian democracy, in his *Construction Construed, and Constitutions Vindicated*. Adams' view of history was that the popular majority always had a tendency to envy the wealth of its betters and use the government to appropriate it, and that this tendency was the chief source of destruction of a free regime. He hoped to avoid the subversion of American republicanism by various devices that would dilute and delay an unwise popular majority: a bicameral legislature with an upper house remote from popular opinion, an executive veto, and an independent judiciary. All Adams' devices have catastrophically failed to limit the federal government and to preserve freedom, as Taylor plainly predicted.

For Taylor, Adams had got his history wrong. The people, in a society like that of Americans, were not dangerous. Most of the time they went quietly about their own business and demanded nothing—unless they were intolerably provoked by abuses of government. It was the "court party" that was the enemy of liberty and that would subvert the free commonwealth. History showed that there were always self-seeking minorities, would-be elites, ready to use the machinery of government to live off the labor of the majority. Sometimes this was done by force, and sometimes by fraud, as in the Hamiltonian maxim "a public debt is a public blessing." The remedy was not to erect artificial "checks and balances" but to make sure power was widely dispersed, limited, and amenable to recall.

The Jeffersonian Constitution has been misrepresented as much as or more than Jeffersonian philosophy. It was not "strict construction," a nonstarter, nor even States' rights. It was State sovereignty. Jefferson (and Madison, too) may be quoted ad infinitum to this effect. The Virginia and Kentucky documents of 1798 – 1800 spell out beyond any doubt that the final defense of freedom in the American system is the people acting in their only constitution-making identity, that of their sovereign states. The states were the legitimate and peaceful resort to protect the liberties of their citizens and themselves as communities from federal encroachment.

Years after leaving the White House, Jefferson writes to an inquisitive foreigner, "But the true barriers of our liberty in this country are our State governments; and the wisest conservative power ever contrived by man, is that of which our Revolution and present government found us possessed. Seventeen distinct States, amalgamated into one as to their foreign concerns, but single and independent as to their internal administration." In the last months of his life, Jefferson suggested to influential Virginians that it was time once again to consider interposing the sovereignty of the state against unconstitutional federal legislation. Never for a day in his life did Jefferson doubt that the people of a state could exercise their sovereignty by leaving the Union, though it was not something to be encouraged rashly. He rather expected that the expanding country would break up into two or more confederacies. That was fine if it was what the people wanted. Americans were rightly joined together by fellow feeling—shared blood and sacrifice—not by the armed force of Washington City.

Commentators have twisted themselves into incredible acrobatic postures and wholesaled semi-plausible lies to assert that Jefferson did not really mean the plain language of what he said. Others have "explained" that Jeffersonian States' rights was only a temporary and expedient device to defend liberty, a device now made unnecessary by modern liberalisms defense of dissent. They miss the point, unwelcome to all adherents of elitist agendas and centralized power—for Jefferson, individual liberty and state sovereignty were indivisible. Properly rebellious free men defended themselves and their communities from Leviathan.

The eclipse of the Jeffersonian preference for limited power and economic freedom had less to do with politics than it did with changes in the spirit of society as the 19th century progressed. Almost from the first days of the United States, New England leadership undertook to establish the New England way as the true and only American way. This was carried out in politics, religion, education, literature, historical writing, and even in lexicography, with vigor and persistence. This is a subject worthy of a multi volume study of a phenomenon that is unrecognized today, although it was a decisive event in our history and clearly understood while it was taking place.

The Puritan conquest of the North was not as easy as has been thought, but was accomplished by about 1850. James Fenimore Cooper in his Littlepage trilogy describes and laments how the unique Anglo-Dutch society of old New York was transformed by the swarm of hustling immigrants from east of the Hudson. Meanwhile, Emerson went to Europe and absorbed the Germanized version of the French Revolution, which was really just going back to his Puritan roots. He came home a Unitarian. The mission was changed, but the intensity of the need to correct the world to conform to the New England plan remained the same. It soon brought to heel the Northwest and the unruly Catholic immigrants.

The South was a different matter. It had developed from a different base and in a different way. Southerners were proud and determined to do it their way, individually and as a people. The South could not be converted or subverted, so it had to be destroyed, the grapes of wrath had to be trampled out. A 30-year campaign of slander and hatred, combined with economic developments, finally brought on in 1861 the circumstances in which this could be accomplished. Americans like to think that their campaign for the abolition of slavery was all about benevolence and liberty. A bit of genuine historical research into what they actually said at the time paints a different picture. The Yankees hated slavery because the slaves were a non-Anglo-Saxon element who had, in their view, hopelessly corrupted white Southerners. In the slaveholding society, white men had far too much liberty and independent power. Such liberty offended puritan sensibilities and created an evil disposition to thwart New England economic and cultural hegemony. It was not that the black man had too little liberty; it was that the Southern white man had far too much liberty and was abusing it by his alleged laziness and immorality.

That crusade led to more than "a little rebellion." Its defeat pretty well finished off Jeffersonian democracy. As Gen. R.E. Lee wrote to Lord Acton the year after his surrender, "the consolidation of the States into one vast republic, sure to be aggressive abroad and despotic at home," was the precursor of American ruin. Lincoln rightly remains the truly representative American. He is the symbol of the highly successful synthesis of capitalist oligarchy, puritan conformity and hypocrisy, and perpetual social revolution from the top down that is the mainstream of American life. There are many who find that synthesis beautiful, though most often they do not really understand what it is, identifying with one or another of the elements and not with the combination itself. Money rules and permits a politics that consists almost entirely of sham battles between the old puritans, the "conservatives," and the secular ones, the "liberals." From time to time they all join together in a messianic war to destroy the latest menace to Lincoln's vision: the South, the Kaiser, the Red Menace, drugs, terror, white privilege, homophobia, etc.

They share the sense that the meaning of "America" is a mission to bring the abstract ideals of the American standard to all mankind. A Jeffersonian, if any still existed, would insist that Americans are not here to be used for anybody's mission, and the proper point of reference is what is good for them. And they have the right to defend that good from Government.

The Jeffersonian spirit survived for a while underground, and now and then a weak and confused revival occurred, as in the days of William Jennings Bryan and populism. The last significant appearance was perhaps the agrarian, non-Marxist critique of capitalism in the 1930's. Nowhere to be seen now are the old Jeffersonians, once a major American type, rebellious men who dared defend the rights of themselves and their communities from outside impositions. But buried somewhere deep in the American soul is a tiny ember of Jeffersonian democracy that now and then gives off an uncertain, feeble, and futile spark.

Clyde Wilson proudly reports that one of his ancestors took part in Bacon's Rebellion in 1676.

4.

A Serpent in Eden

All things at Rome are for sale.—Juvenal

THOMAS JEFFERSON HAS LEFT US an account of a supper table conversation in the very earliest days of the U.S. government. He considered it significant enough to make a record of it.

Vice-President John Adams (who was intended by nature for a professor) declaimed at length about the virtues of the British government, which, he said, if purged of its corruption, would be perfection. Secretary of the Treasury Alexander Hamilton (a canny immigrant bastard with a Napoleon complex) differed sharply. It was its corruption, he avowed, that gave the British government its great stability and power.

When Jefferson heard Hamilton declare that "a public debt is a public blessing" he knew he had spotted the serpent in Eden.

Adams and Hamilton were Federalists. They wanted to give the government a nationalist cast that violated the federalist Constitution which had been ratified and their own previous statements in securing ratification.

Also, they believed that in America the people could not be denied a role in government, however unwise that might be. The people, fortunately, were usually an inert mass, but they could become dangerous. They might discover that they could vote themselves the wealth of their betters. So things had to be properly arranged. The people could have their say in a Commons, but the government needed a powerful executive above the people to give it initiative and force. With some justice Jefferson referred to the Federalists as "monarchy men."

As President Adams was obsessed with titles and ceremonies. President Jefferson, a genuine aristocrat, avoided ostentatious trappings of office. As Adams saw it, to his credit, good government required also an upper house of Senators (republican Lords) which had two essential benefits. It would give status and authority to the wealthy and powerful whose ambitions, as history showed, might otherwise undermine the republic. And it would provide their betters with a check on the expected rash actions of the people.

As the Jeffersonian philosopher John Taylor of Caroline pointed out, Adams, in a chimerical pursuit of checks and balances, was trying to create artificial orders where they did not exist.

Further, he did not allow for the circulation of elites that would occur with a growing population settling a vast and nearly empty continent.

Hamilton was right on the mark from his perspective. If you wanted the influence, wealth, and power of society behind a strong and energetic government, you had to make it worth their while. You had to have a British-style public debt—in which an elite class had an interest-bearing claim on government revenue.

The strongest element in the push for a new and stronger federal government with a revenue not dependent on the States had come from the holders of the debts from the War of Independence. By 1789 this debt was not owned by those who had provided goods and services to the cause, but by monied men, chiefly from New York and Philadelphia, who had bought it up at cents on the dollar while it was "not worth a Continental." (One of these was Supreme Court Justice James Wilson who is often touted as a wise "conservative" statesman.) The Continental debt was no longer in the hands of the soldiers and suppliers who had made the Revolution possible. Congressman James Jackson of Georgia observed that there was not a scrap of Continental paper left in his State. Speculators had systematically preyed upon the necessities of the people.

The debt, of course, had to be paid. The centerpiece of Hamilton's initiative was to pay off the debt to its current holders, a number of them members of Congress, at face value in interest-bearing government bonds. Only in this manner could the "good faith and credit" of the government, which was said to be essential, be established. Thus would the wealthy and powerful be embraced in alliance with the government. Before long, Hamilton came up with the scheme of paying off the existing State debts in the same manner as the Continental. There was a difficulty that had to be overcome by political maneuvering. Some of the States, mostly Southern, had already paid off their debts, while some, mostly Northern, had not.

Jeffersonians were often quite intelligent and sophisticated men, but they did not seem to grasp the arcane mysteries of finance. In fact, to them it looked like a bit of a swindle. A public debt at best could only be an onerous necessity in wartime. Who was going to pay that interest to the privileged minority who owned those government bonds? Where else could it come from but the pockets of good folks who actually produced something? It was no spur to prosperity. It merely created what John Taylor called a "paper aristocracy," a class endowed by government with special privilege for which it contributed nothing in return. It reinstated the abuses which the American States had fought a war to be free of.

After all, most of the people were farmers—they produced something real out of the earth with their capital and labour and supplied the overwhelming bulk of American exports that allowed trade with the world. The worthy merchant saw that the farmer's produce was sold and transported and that those things the farmer could not produce for himself were acquired in exchange. The professional man and artisan gave necessary services for which a just compensation was due. Even the manufacturer, when he asked no government bounty and provided goods that could not be found more cheaply elsewhere, played a useful role. (Though no free society could survive when dependent industrial workers became too numerous.) But what exactly did the speculator do for his profits? Nothing except enjoy politically-dictated privilege.

Taylor made a clear moral distinction between the producer and the speculator, one whose occupation was to manipulate paper for the acquisition of wealth produced by other men. Economists will doubtless find this a naive idea, and libertarians will avow that the speculator is a legitimate contributor to the smooth workings of the free market. But it is a very basic question getting toward the proper nature of a good regime. Could we learn anything useful for our present troubles by applying the distinction between producer and speculator?

Further, as Taylor argued with length, breadth, and depth, the whole Federalist case was based on a false understanding of society. The masses preying on the wealth of the classes was fairly infrequent in history. The masses were generally content merely to enjoy their modest own. The norm of history was that the classes preyed on the earnings of the masses. This was done either by force or by fraud—and the British/Hamiltonian public debt ("the funds" as it was called in England) was the latest fad in frauds, covering up extortion by the mysteries of finance.

The Jeffersonians asked some very fundamental questions that have had no hearing since Lincoln, about things that have long now been taken for granted as normal. Why should the government, which has an immense income of its own, have to borrow money and pay interest to private persons at all? (Of course, deficits were not expected to become ordinary.) The government might pay its expenses by issuing notes, redeemable promises to pay. These would not need to be made arbitrary legal tender because they rested on the government's credit. Furthermore, since they were sound, they could circulate as money, providing a convenience and fulfilling the Constitutional requirement to regulate the currency. What did borrowing money from the rich in the form of interest-bearing bonds amount to except a guaranteed risk-free profit to certain well-connected interests? Throughout the 19th century, when Treasury notes were proposed, the bankers, with the customary Whig-Republican dishonesty, raised the cry that the people would be forced to use the government's money instead of the "people's" (i.e., bankers') money. It was an unthinkable invasion of the people's rights!

The public debt was thus bound up with the question of banking and currency, as Hamilton well knew when he pushed for a "national" bank—actually a private corporation in which the government invested and to which the government delegated certain privileges. Until Lincoln, politicians argued ad nauseum about bank or no—bank, seldom touching the real question—that is, who would control the money supply. Secretary of the Treasury Hamilton quietly did something more significant than the national bank—he issued an executive order by which the government would accept as if they were gold, the paper notes issued by private banks controlled by his friends and supporters.

The love of it is the root of much evil and yet the desire for it is nearly universal. More, money is a mystery. What is it, where does it come from, why does it increase or decrease in value? Banks, it seems, and government are somehow involved in the answers to these questions. I have been studying this subject as closely as I could for more than forty years. I know enough to know that I do not understand it. I know enough to know that politicians and journalists haven't a clue, and enough to doubt that most economists understand it. It is possible that some financiers understand it, but why should they let us in on their immensely profitable knowledge?

And historians are no better since they generally repeat the deceptive party polemics of the past and don't have any idea what was really going on. For example, it is said that Andrew Jackson fought the national bank because he hated paper money and wanted a sound specie currency. Yes, that is what he thought he was doing. The Philadelphia national bank, though unconstitutional and a dangerous grant of power to private interests, actually kept the circulating paper of the country sound, something which Martin Van Buren's bankers in New York felt cramped their style. Once the national bank was out of the way, they started loaning out paper notes with gay abandon. The original issuers of unbacked paper make a profit out of the air. As they circulate, the notes lose value. Why then don't depositors present their bad paper to the banks and demand specie, a puzzled French free market philosopher Frederic Bastiat asked the great pioneer American economist Condy Raguet? Because the depositors know that the banks will retaliate by cutting off their credit and calling in their loans. So, Jackson's ill-advised (and illegal and arbitrary) actions against the national bank resulted not in a hard money economy but in destructive inflation.

The trouble with judging economic policies is that sequences are not always consequences. And the variables are many and large. The air is full of the claims of politicians that their virtues have caused prosperity or the errors of their rivals have harmed the people. And the claims of "experts" that their wisdom is responsible for good outcomes. Most of what passes for public discussion of economic policy is irresponsibly ignorant assertions or self-serving lies. One might call the debate juvenile if "childish" were not an even more accurate label. Remember, we are talking here about that mysterious thing, the love of which is universal and the root of much evil. As the old saying goes: "It takes brass to get gold." If you are good at it, swindling is a lot more profitable and fun than work. Hamiltonians lived by this rule.

What passes for generally accepted history of American banking and currency, I am convinced, is as off-base as the account of Jackson and the Monster Bank—greenbacks, legal tender, the gold/silver ratio, the Federal Reserve are all described in terms of deceptive party rhetoric, when the real question was: which set of scoundrels gets to work the game? True, the Federal Reserve is an atrocity, giving a private banking cartel the power to expand and contract the money supply, which means potential control of everything. But the Federal Reserve, truly conspiratorial and outrageous, is only a concentrated version of Lincoln's more dispersed national banking cartel. The essential issue is deeper. Who has the right to control the money supply and credit of our immense economy, and what should they rightly do with that power?

With the third part of his program, direct subsidy of business and "protective" tariffs on imports to guarantee manufacturers a captive domestic market, Hamilton had less immediate success than with public debt and banking. But by the 1820s, agents of the Massachusetts and Pennsylvania industrialists were haunting the lobbies of the Capitol ("lobbyists") to buy Congressmen to vote "protection" for their "infant industries" (i.e., import taxes to exclude their foreign competition and allow them to sell at the highest possible prices). Even Hamilton would have been shocked by the 30% tariff of the Abomination Act of 1828 and the 50% rate in the Morrill Act of 1861. It is estimated that iron and steel tariffs added $6,000 per mile to the cost of railroad construction in the 19th century. Is it any wonder that Congressman Thaddeus Stevens of Pennsylvania, who happened also to be an iron magnate, wanted a permanent Reconstruction that would keep the South forever without political power?

The case for tariff "protection" for American industry was and is based on the claim that it makes for national independence and self-sufficiency, and that it was responsible for American prosperity and high wages. How can forcing everyone to pay higher prices than necessary for what they buy be a cause of prosperity? Tariffs do not create wealth, they shift it around and make some people more prosperous. The great advance in industry and wealth in the United States during the 19th and early 20th centuries was a result of a hardworking, innovative population turned loose on a vast cornucopia of natural resources, not the product of tariff legislation cunningly crafted to benefit some at the expense of others. Indeed, the tariff probably slowed development.

Again, Jeffersonians asked the right questions. They really believed in free enterprise.

Adam Smith pointed out the general truth that free trade in goods between individuals of different countries, taking the benefit of comparative advantage, was good for his country and, indeed for mankind in general. His country was a given, and free trade could be of more use to it than government meddling. Exchanging goods without interference was one thing. Selling off the country is something else. Neither Smith nor the Jeffersonian anti-tariff Americans of the 19th century saw free trade as the international manipulation of money and labour-arbitrage that sacrifices citizens to foreigners for private profit (a modern version of the international slave trade). The speculators of our day have taken their game into realms remote from the benefit of their country and its producers. They trade not in goods but in people, while they gamble on pieces of paper (or rather cyber entries).

Economics as practiced today is a utilitarian and materialistic study. It is concerned with maximizing profit, with describing the actions of man as an economic being, and explaining the allegedly inevitable results of supposed economic laws. Our Jeffersonian forebears did not practice economics. They practiced political economy—which is concerned with human well-being. Those old-time Southerners who fought against Hamilton and Lincoln did not assume that man is to be understood wholly or chiefly as an economic being. They did not believe that the economic conditions they faced were entirely determined by abstract laws—but rather that they were the result of human decisions, some of them the product of corrupt politics. Honourable republican patriots did not put personal profit at the top of their list of the duties of government.

Unlike Marxists and the kinds of capitalists they decried, they did not believe that material conditions controlled the thoughts of man. Rather, they believed that the human mind created material conditions. They also did not believe that maximum wealth was the only goal of economic activity. There were such things to be considered as widespread and comfortable prosperity; and stewardship instead of maximum exploitation of God's bounteous Nature. Man must eat, but he does not live by bread alone. Economics being the product of human acts and decisions, it was part of the moral realm and not merely technical knowledge.

Most of all Jeffersonian political economy insisted that the health of society was not represented by great wealth but by widespread ownership of productive property. Without widespread ownership of real property, which made the great mass of men independent citizens, there could be no healthy society, and certainly no free society.

Jefferson did not change over time. We find him remarking: "I believe that banking institutions are more dangerous to our liberties than standing armies." Banknotes were becoming as plentiful and as worthless as oak leaves. After the War of 1812 he writes:

> Like a dropsical man calling out for water, our deluded citizens are clamouring for banks, more banks, The American mind is now in that state of fever which the world has often seen.... We are now taught to believe that legerdemain tricks upon paper can produce as solid wealth as hard labour in the earth. It is vain for common sense to urge that nothing can produce but nothing.

This is a real and long-lasting tradition of thought. It was basic to Thomas Jefferson's opposition to the economic program of Alexander Hamilton. The tradition is fully explicated in the writings of John Taylor of Caroline and in the speeches of John C. Calhoun and many other Southern statesmen. The tradition was expressed in provisions of the Confederate Constitution.

5.

JEFFERSON AND STATE INTERPOSITION

"Resolved, That the several States composing the United States of America, are not united on the principle of unlimited submission to their General Government.... and that whensoever the General Government assumes undelegated powers, its acts are unauthoritative, void, and of no force.... that the government created by this compact [the Constitution for the United States] was not made the exclusive or final judge of the extent of the powers delegated to itself; since that would have made its discretion, and not the Constitution, the measure of its powers; that this would be to surrender the form of government we have chosen, and live under one deriving its powers from its own will, and not from our authority;... and that the co-States, recurring to their natural right in cases not made federal, will concur in declaring these acts void, and of no force, and will each take measures of its own for providing that neither these acts, nor any others of the General Government not plainly and intentionally authorised by the Constitution, shall be exercised within their respective territories."

SO WROTE THOMAS JEFFERSON, Vice President of the United States, in a document drafted at the request of members of the Kentucky legislature in 1798. Kentucky adopted Jefferson's paper and broadcast it to the world as the definitive opinion and stand of the sovereign people of the State. The language drafted by James Madison for companion documents adopted by the Virginia legislature in 1799 and 1800 was similarly unequivocal in its constitutional position.

The people, acting through their natural polities, the States, had created and given authority to the Constitution of the United States. The Constitution conferred powers on a general government to handle certain specified matters that were common to the "general welfare" of all the States. That government was an agent. It could not be the judge of its own powers. To allow it to be so would mean nothing less than a government of unlimited power, a tyranny. The partners to the Constitution, the sovereign peoples of the States, were the final judges of what they had intended the Constitution to mean. When the general government exceeded its power it was the right and duty of the State to interpose its authority and defend its people from federal acts of tyranny—yes, to render a federal law inoperative in the State's jurisdiction.

The scholars of the rising leftist Establishment who took over American history writing beginning in the 1930s invented a self-flattering fable to render the Kentucky and Virginia documents themselves null and void. Jefferson and Madison, they said, really did not care about States' rights. They were merely anticipating the great tradition of liberalism. Their concern was to defend the freedom of speech of the non-conformist radicals of their time. In their minds, Jefferson and Madison could not possibly have advocated such an un-Lincolnian thing as state sovereignty.

This established interpretation is a lie and requires a good deal of either ignorance, self-deception, or deliberate falsehood to peddle. It is true that the Virginia and Kentucky acts were not followed up by active resistance to the feds. They did not have to be, because Jefferson and his friends won the following elections, got rid of the bad laws, and compensated those who had been harmed by them. There is evidence that Virginia and North Carolina were quite willing and able to call out the militia if necessary and that grand juries were standing by to indict any offending feds.

Not interested in State rights? Jefferson reiterated the centrality of State rights to the preservation of liberty and self-government in his inaugural address (and in many letters for the rest of his life). His party and the succeeding Democratic party proclaimed "The Principles of 1798" repeatedly as their foundational philosophy, right up to the War to Prevent Southern Independence. It could not be clearer: in the American government system State rights and liberty could not be separated. They were the same thing. They had the same defenders and the same enemies. The Sedition Act was not just an invasion of individual rights, it was an illegal invasion of a sphere that the people had left to their States.

Further, the Sedition Act, punishing criticism of federal officials with jail sentences and fines, had been passed in stark defiance of the recently adopted First and Tenth Amendments which absolutely forbade Congress to pass any law abridging the freedom of speech and press and reserved to the States all powers not specifically conferred on the government. How then could Congress pass such a law as the Sedition Act? Because the Federalists, Hamilton and Adams and their supporters, justified their legislation by invoking the Common Law's provisions about the punishment of "sedition." The Common Law existed in each State to the extent that the State had found it worthwhile to adopt it, but it had no place in a written agreement of delegated powers such as the Constitution for the United States. If the Federalists could ignore specified power limitations by grafting Common Law jurisdiction into the Constitution, then literally everything under the sun could be brought under their power. Not only that, but everything under the sun could be ultimately disposed of by the federal courts, which would become the new sovereign. This had to be stopped.

Interposition by Virginia and Kentucky was intended to halt the Northeastern elite's relentless agenda to become the economic and moral overseers of all Americans through the federal machine. This has always been the engine for the unconstitutional usurpation of federal power—then, since, and now. When State interposition next came into serious play in the United States, the occasion was the tariff laws, by which the Northeastern elite had perverted a constitutional power to raise a revenue into a means of excluding foreign competition and creating a captive market for their profit.

After their service as presidents, Jefferson and Madison lived by their republican ethics—they were private citizens with no special right to interfere in public affairs. But they expressed opinions on issues of the day privately to those who asked and who they trusted. When, less than a generation after the "Principles of 1798" had been proclaimed, the possible nullification of the tariff laws by South Carolina drew attention, Jefferson was gone from the scene. Madison, in contradiction of his own plain language and the circumstances of 1798—1800, claimed that state interposition was not what they had had in mind at that time. Historians who want to trash States' rights and the South Carolina resistance to the tariff during 1828—1833 lean heavily on Madison's somewhat vague statements. Self-evidently, Madison contradicted himself, as he did quite often throughout his career. Unlike Jefferson, he was superficial and an inconsistent thinker who often swung from one side to the other. That is why his pretentious speculations in *The Federalist*, which, by his own admission, have absolutely no constitutional authority whatsoever, are the favourite text of third string "constitutional lawyers" and would-be "political philosophers."

We do not have to wonder what Jefferson in his post-presidential years thought about State interposition. It is not in the least a mystery, although it is something of a secret since "scholars" have assiduously avoided exposure of the relevant documents, which are not easy to find. In 1825, the day after his last

Christmas in this earthly realm, Jefferson wrote to William Branch Giles, former Governor of Virginia and stalwart Jeffersonian. He shared Giles's concerns about the state of federal affairs:

> I see, as you do, and with the deepest affliction, the rapid strides with which the federal branch of the government is advancing towards the usurpation of all the rights reserved to the States, and the consolidation in itself of all powers, foreign and domestic; and that, too, by constructions which, if legitimate, leave no limits to their powers.

The minority President John Quincy Adams was pushing a large program of federal expenditures and expanded powers. Adams and his Congressional allies, Jefferson said, for example, had construed the delegated power to establish post roads into a power to cut down mountains and dig canals. The old, evil program of the Northeastern "monarchists" to enrich themselves off the earnings of the agriculturalists was once again in the saddle. Reason and argument were no good in such a situation. *"You might as well reason and argue with the marble columns"* in the Capitol.

The South might well be forced into a choice between *"the dissolution of the Union with them or submission to a government without limitation of powers. Between these two evils, when we must make a choice, there can be no hesitation. But in the meanwhile, the States should be watchful to note every material usurpation on their rights; to denounce them as they occur in the most peremptory terms, to protest them as wrongs to which our present submission shall be considered, not as acknowledgments..."* In other words, recur to the Kentucky Resolutions.

Jefferson mentioned that he had written a letter to Giles on Christmas about important matters, of which Giles "will be free to make use what you please." I have not found this letter, but it may have something to do with a document Jefferson wrote out on

December 24, which he titled "The Solemn Declaration and Protest of the Citizens of Virginia on the Principles of the Constitution of the United States of America and the Violation of Them." It seems to have been intended for the use of Jefferson's neighbours in the grand jury of Albemarle County to begin a program for Virginia once more to interpose, against Congress's usurpation in its "internal improvements" expenditures.

Just three years after Jefferson wrote this, another Vice-President of the United States, at the request of his State, drafted a "South Carolina Exposition," which described the illegality and injustice of the protective tariff and the proper remedy for it: State interposition upon "The Principles of 1798." This "Exposition" was approved and broadcast to the world by the legislature of South Carolina, along with a "Protest." The usual clamour of rent-seekers and petty political operators was raised, claiming, among other things, that Jefferson had not written the Kentucky Resolutions. In 1831, Jefferson's son-in-law produced the draft in the great man's own hand.

There was so much demagogurey broadcast by the opponents of nullification and the shoddy historians who repeat their propaganda, that it is worth saying something about the roles of Jefferson and Calhoun as drafters of the Kentucky Resolutions and the South Carolina Exposition. Jefferson, as we have noted, did not publicly acknowledge his authorship. Calhoun's anonymous authorship of the Exposition was characterised as an evil, secretive political operation. This propaganda is designed by and for people who can think only in terms of politicians and parties instead of principles and are ignorant of the ethics of republican virtue that influenced many Americans before Lincoln. Authorship was not acknowledged in both cases because it was desired that the statements be understood as the voice of the people of the State, not mischaracterised as merely the position of a national politician.

In a later generation, a minority president seemingly destroyed forever the constitutional role of the States by declaring the open, democratic, deliberative acts of fourteen States to be only "combinations" of criminals who refused to obey him. Lincoln made that stick by a brutal war of conquest that did not "preserve the Union" but changed the Union into a central state with no limits to its power. Those who hope to revive a constitutional role for the States as counters to the present U.S. Empire, must hope to make the States once more into self-conscious, viable polities who have the political will to enact nullification and stand by it. As Taylor of Caroilne remarked: "There are no rights where there are no remedies."

6.

JEFFERSON AND AFRICAN AMERICAN SLAVERY

THOMAS JEFFERSON'S FUNDAMENTAL IDENTITY was as a Virginia planter. It is impossible to imagine him as anything else, although I suspect that 20th century liberals are incapable of thinking of him other than as someone like themselves. He was born into the upper ranks of and spent his lifetime in a society in which the holding of black bonded people in household slavery had been legal and customary for over a century.

Until his later years he was an optimist who believed that enlightenment could lead to a better world, including the removal of slavery, a contradiction in a republican society. He was not a zealot. He lived at ease among slaves who at one time reached 200 in number. There were no barbed wire or armed guards around Monticello. Perhaps there surrounded him the normal amount of human happiness and unhappiness that is to be expected for mankind in this vale of tears.

Slavery was a major element of the Virginia economy, and the production of tobacco was the mainstay of American exports. Forty percent of the Virginia population were slaves. They were a majority in South Carolina and were legally present in all the thirteen colonies including ten percent in New York and nearly as many in Connecticut and Rhode Island. Only Quakers made an open appeal for emancipation and the slave population of the North was actually increasing prior to the Revolution.

Jefferson on more than one occasion deplored the existence of slavery as an unhealthy element of society. In this he was in company with a strong segment of American and of Southern opinion. With this difference: while Jefferson and most Southerners thought slavery bad in principle, Northern opponents of slavery believed it was bad economics, unfairly increased Southern political influence, and hated the presence of black people in America.

The Declaration of Independence had cited as a grievance against the king that he had held open the importation of slaves in the interest of British companies after Virginia had several times petitioned that importations be closed and then he encouraged the slaves to revolt against their American masters. In fact, there was little need for more Africans to be brought in because the slave population was proliferating mightily by natural increase—a sign of relatively good conditions. Jefferson was a sponsor of the Northwest Ordinance of 1785 by which slavery was prohibited in that vast territory that Virginia had conquered and generously given to the people of all the colonies for settlement. At that time the foreign slave trade was still wide open and would remain so until 1808. The Constitution had not been adopted and there was no issue of the status of slavery in a sovereign state. In fact, in the 1820s, Illinois, which had been a part of the Northwest Territory, seriously debated legalising slave-holding. The treaties acquiring the Louisiana Territory and Florida guaranteed the property of the French and Spanish inhabitants.

Early on Jefferson proposed an emancipation plan for Virginia. It got nowhere. His proposal was that slaves born after a certain date would be freed at adulthood and trained to be self-supporting. Then the State would send them away, well-equipped, to "be colonised in such a place as the circumstances of the time should render most proper." He recognised that such colonies would probably have to be supported and administered by Virginians for some time into the future.

In his well-known Query XIV of *Notes on the State of Virginia*, published in 1787 though written earlier, Jefferson reiterated his belief that slavery had a baneful effect, particularly upon the white people of a free commonwealth. He discussed at length the question of whether the white and black races were equal, deciding that there was probably an unbridgeable inferiority in intelligence and difference in temperament which emancipation would not remove. He hoped that slavery could be eliminated. But a second step would be required "unknown to history," because emancipation in the ancient world had not required absorption of an alien race..."When freed, he is to be removed beyond the reach of mixture." This was essentially the same answer to slavery given by Abraham Lincoln, who had no idea what to do about slavery except use it as political propaganda to aid his career, proclaiming emancipation in the worst possible way and only when it became a useful support to his war of invasion and conquest.

Slavery extended naturally into the new states to which Southern families migrated, and such States joined the Union without any question until 1819. In that year a majority in the House of Representatives attempted to prevent the admission of Missouri, from the Louisiana Purchase and settled largely by people from Virginia and Kentucky, unless it changed the constitution adopted by the people to eliminate slaveholding. This issue, though temporarily compromised, embroiled Congress and the American people in a recurrent bitter controversy over what was called "the extension of slavery." The ultimate result of the controversy was secession.

In 1860, Lincoln's party called for prohibiting what it termed "the extension of slavery" into the territory acquired by the Mexican War. The party called itself Republican after Thomas Jefferson's party on the grounds of Jefferson's support of the Northwest Ordinance. This was a presumptuous act of deceit, especially since the new Republican party represented the polar opposite of Jeffersonian economic policies and its core consisted of the Yankee-derived elements of the American population which had viciously opposed him.

Let's see what the retired elder statesman Thomas Jefferson had to say about the "extension of slavery." To his old friend Lafayette he explained the Missouri controversy as "a trick of hypocrisy" on the part of the monarchy men he had put down in 1800, explaining:

> On the eclipse of federalism with us, although not its extinction, its leaders got up the Missouri question, under the false front of lessening the measure of slavery, but with the real view of producing a geographical division of parties, which might ensure them the next president. The people of the north went blind fold into the snare...

James Madison and Charles Pinckney, among the last surviving members of the Constitutional Convention, agreed with Jefferson's appraisal of the Missouri question. In 1820, Jefferson wrote his thanks to John Holmes, a Northerner who had supported the Southern position in Congress:

> I had for a long time ceased to read newspapers or pay any attention to public affairs. But this momentous question, like a fire-bell in the night, awakened and filled me with terror. I considered it at once as the knell of the Union. It is hushed, indeed, for the moment. But this is a reprieve only, not a final sentence. A geographical line, coinciding with a marked principle, moral and political, once conceived and held up to the angry passions of men, will never be obliterated; and every new irritation will mark it deeper and deeper. I can say, with conscious truth,

that there is not a man on earth who would sacrifice more than I would to relieve us from this heavy reproach, in any practicable way...The cession of that kind of property, for so it is misnamed, is a bagatelle which would not cost me a second thought, if, in that way, a general emancipation and expatriation could be affected; and gradually, with due sacrifices, I think it might be.

But, as it is, we have the wolf by the ears, and we can neither hold him, nor safely let him go. Justice is in one scale, and self-preservation in the other. Of one thing I am certain, that as the passage of slaves from one State to another, would not make a slave of a single human being who would not be so without it, so their diffusion over a greater surface would make them individually happier, and proportionally facilitate the accomplishment of their emancipation, by dividing the burden on a greater number of coadjutors. An abstinence too, from this act of power, would remove the jealousy excited by the undertaking of Congress to regulate the different descriptions of men composing a State. This is certainly the exclusive right of every State, which nothing in the Constitution has taken from them and given to the General Government....

I regret that I am now to die in the belief, that the useless sacrifice of themselves by the generation of 1776, to acquire self-government and happiness to their country, is to be thrown away by the unwise and unworthy passions of their sons, and my only consolation is to be, that I live not to weep over it. If they would but dispassionately weigh the blessings they will throw away, against an abstract principle more likely to be effected by union than by scission, they would pause before they would perpetrate this act of suicide on themselves, and of treason against the hopes of the world.

At the time of the Missouri controversy, John Adams wrote Jefferson that he was happy to leave the question of slavery to Southern men. Besides, he pointed out, "slave" was just a word while the condition of the labouring poor in the North could scarcely be differentiated from that of Southern blacks.

In an earlier almost unnoticed discussion of labour in 1814, Jefferson wrote:

> Nor in the class of labourers do I mean to withhold from comparison that portion whose colour has condemned them, in certain parts of our Union, to a subjection to the will of others. Even these are better fed in these States, warmer clothed, and labour less than the journeymen or day labourers of England. They have the comfort, too, of numerous families in the midst of whom they live without want, or fear of it; a solace which few of the labourers of England possess. They are subject, it is true, to bodily coercion; but are not the hundreds of thousands of British soldiers and seamen subject to the same, without seeing, at the end of their career... the certainty which the other has, that he will never want? And has not the British seaman, as much as the African, been reduced to this bondage by force, in flagrant violation of his own consent, and of his natural right in his own person? And with the labourers of England generally, does not the moral coercion of want subject their will as despotically to that of their employer as does the physical restraint does the soldier, the seaman, or the slave?

Jefferson added that by his comparison he did not mean to endorse any form of coerced labour—equally condemned the European and American reality.

For Jefferson, the stand against the "extension of slavery," which would later bring Lincoln into power, was insincere and counterproductive. It violated State sovereignty and the consent of the governed, would destroy the Union, and benefited only Northern politicians and rent-seekers with a disguised power-and-profit agenda. Note that it was not slavery that Jefferson identified as the death knell of the Union, as has sometimes been asserted, but the Northern campaign against slavery. And yet the standard nationalist account of United States history makes Abraham Lincoln the heir of Thomas Jefferson's mission against slavery and Southerners wicked traitors to Jefferson's legacy. Rather, Lincoln's stand against slavery, becomes in the light of Jefferson's true position an irresponsible provocation and a default on the North's share of the burden of emancipation.

7.

Looking For Jeffersonian Democracy

Your people are a great beast.—Alexander Hamilton

Then there are the deplorables.—Hillary Clinton

THOMAS JEFFERSON REMAINS the best American symbol for democracy—that is, decision-making by majority rule of the body of citizens. He really believed in the rule of the people. In the short run they might go astray, but the people—with their judgment, honesty, and patriotism—were the best reliance for a good commonwealth. That is why he was admired and popular in his own time and later, and why more towns, counties, and schools were named for him than even Washington.

You see it in the first inaugural address. On another occasion he writes: "I am not among those who fear the people. They, and not the rich, are our dependence for continued freedom." He asks: if, as the Federalists say, man is flawed and cannot be trusted to govern himself, then "where do those angels come from" who are especially endowed to govern others?

He does not regard majority rule as sacred, but only thinks that a majority is more likely to make a just decision than any self-appointed wise and good. This seems to me a definitive response to elitism. And it brings to mind what C.S. Lewis and Churchill had to say about democracy: it is not perfect but it is better than anything else that has been tried.

Two qualifying points here are necessary for 21st century readers. First, in Jefferson's ideal most of life and society was outside the jurisdiction of government of any kind. The majority ruled in a very limited sphere. They were not entitled to do anything they wanted. They could not make coercive transfers of wealth or force changes in society to suit some plan of supposed improvement.

Second, Jefferson always has in mind a known commonwealth like Virginia. His majority consists of citizens who have a stake in the commonwealth for themselves and their posterity—men who head families, pay taxes, and serve in the militia.

Of course, Americans have long taken to heart Lincoln's pretty words about saving government of, by and for the people. Traditional self-righteousness long ago abandoned facts and distorted understanding. Lincoln, who 60% of the people voted against, turned his office into a juggernaut making war upon quite a large number of people who did not consent to his rule.

Lincoln's evocation of the people renders them a rather vague, unspecific, and malleable category detached from the real people of America. It justifies any group of politicians who manage to win an election and pretend to speak for "the people."

Jeffersonian democracy looms large in history and has been misinterpreted and misused so long and so pervasively that it is immensely important to get Jefferson right. He provides a near perfect test case of the distortion of American history. Jefferson was extraordinary, but he is also representative of many things that have been broadly shared by his fellow Americans before, during, and after his own time.

Taylor of Caroline asks, What are the People? Tariff legislation profiting a few Northeastern factory owners at everyone else's expense becomes an "American System" promising prosperity to We the People. And "Americans" are said to have a duty to expend our lives and treasure bringing democracy to foreign peoples (whether they want it or not). Where is that in the powers bestowed on the federal government by the Constitution? Since they are conveniently vague and malleable, We the People is all of us who have the obligation but not really any of us individually. Its effect is merely to claim the benediction of We the People for every increase in the wealth and power of the rulers.

Despite the hysterical propaganda of New Englanders, Jefferson was no Jacobin. He spoke for a few small changes in Virginia society that he thought might increase and secure liberty. Albert Jay Nock's biography has a revealing incident. Mobs are fighting in the streets of Paris. The mobs part and allow the American minister's carriage to pass through peacefully.

Majority rule, of course, had to be as close to the people as possible. In a little noticed remark, Jefferson wrote: "To safeguard democracy, the people must have a keen sense of independence, self-respect, and oneness." "Oneness" implies a cohesion that does not fit well with a drive for "diversity." Virginia provided his oneness.

When Jefferson left the White House in 1809, he had to ford seven rivers and creeks to get home. He lived another 17 years and never left Virginia. His public activities during that time were entirely concerned with Virginia. He was quick to defend Virginia's reputation from New England's efforts to claim all credit for the War of Independence.

Two years before his death he wrote this to an Englishman:

> Virginia, of which I am myself a native and resident, was not only the first of the States but, I believe I may say, the first of the nations of the earth, which assembled its wise men peacefully together to form

a fundamental constitution, to commit it to writing, and place it among the archives, where everyone should be free to appeal to its text.

When Jefferson returned from his diplomatic service in France, the ship in which he sailed contained carefully packed and preserved samples of every plant useful or potentially useful to Virginia that he had encountered in Europe. His only book, *Notes on the State of Virginia*, was prompted by a wish to counter erroneous European notions about his homeland.

Liberty being dependent on the closeness of the people to government and the necessity of their oneness led Jefferson to one of his more speculative recommendations—administration divided into townships or "hundreds." This proposal to bring government as close as possible to the people has been admired by some but lacked Jefferson's usual solid grounding. It was too artificial and too remote from what the people were accustomed to.

Jeffersonianism was formed in the political conflicts of the 1790s. Indeed, the political ideas of the South, though having deep roots, were made explicit by Jefferson and his friends in their opposition to the agenda of Alexander Hamilton and John Adams. Through American history—right up to today—one must, I suggest, be for Hamilton or for Jefferson. Hamilton has ruled for a long time now, but unless we properly know Jefferson we will never understand American history.

The triumph of Hamilton over Jefferson means that the American spirit changed from republican idealism to Calvin Coolidge's maxim that "the business of America is business. "

The aggressive actions of the Hamiltonians almost as soon as the new government was inaugurated was a cluster of corruptions that needed paring away, just like the cumulative abuses that had led the thirteen colonies to fight for independence. The centralists had been defeated in the Constitutional Convention and in the ratification by the States, but they set to it at once to reinterpret the Constitution to suit their purposes. Instead of just paying off the war debt they turned it into a permanent necessity for taxation so that the wealthy and well-placed could enjoy risk-free interest-bearing bonds. Although the Philadelphia Convention had refused to give the new government a right to charter corporations, the Hamiltonians soon had a national bank which they justified under the "necessary and proper" phrase in the Constitution. It was not a government bank but a private cartel which enjoyed the immense power and profit of Congress's responsibility to regulate the currency. They imposed needless direct taxes to make their power felt by the people and a treaty which sacrificed the interests of Southern and western farmers to the greed of New England. As Jefferson said, the livelihood of the South was threatened by abuses and its feelings were constantly insulted.

Worst of all perhaps was the Sedition Act, under which newspaper editors were fined and jailed for criticism of President Adams. How could this happen under a constitution that specifically prevented the government from interfering with freedom of the press? The centralists simply assumed, preposterously, that the Constitution should be interpreted through the English Common Law, and that law justified the punishment of sedition.

In the 1790s, Vice-President John Adams fortified his house in fear that the American rabble might imitate the French and attack him, while Jefferson lived at ease among his 200 slaves. As President Adams rode about in a carriage with four white horses and insisted on being addressed as "Your Excellency." When Jefferson became President he walked to his inauguration in plain dress. Further, he sent his annual message to the houses of Congress in writing, setting an example of simple unostentatious republican virtue in place of the President delivering his message to deferential legislators like a monarch. Jefferson's custom continued until the 20th century, when the United States, now the United State of the American Empire, returned to the royal ritual. And when Jefferson entertained at the White House he ignored all the European nonsense about precedence and hierarchy and conducted himself like the gentlemanly host of any Virginia country supper, offering his arm to the nearest lady and encouraging all to follow suit.

It is a simple truth that there would have been no Jeffersonian democracy without the South. A fact either ignored, disguised or decried these days. The same is true of "Jacksonian democracy," as a brief glance at voting statistics will demonstrate. Jefferson, Madison, and Monroe occupied the Presidency longer than all the Northerners put together before 1860.

American leaders before Lincoln were, like Jefferson, Southern plantation owners in their primary social identity. Broadly speaking, Jeffersonianism represented the majority agricultural interest and its opposition the commercial and monied interest.

In 1798, two years before he was elected President of the United States, Jefferson wrote his ally John Taylor that it

> ...was not unusual now to estimate the separate mass of Virginia and North Carolina, with a view to their separate existence. It is true that we are completely under the saddle of Massachusetts and Connecticut, and that they ride us very hard, cruelly insulting our feelings, as well as exhausting our strength and subsistence.

He continued with a description of New Englanders: "They are circumscribed within such narrow limits...and they are marked... with such a perversity of character, as to constitute, from that circumstance, the natural division of our parties."

He had said the same thing to President Washington a few years before when he had resigned from the first Cabinet: there was a faction hiding behind Washington that was perverting the Constitution that had been ratified to create a central state controlled by a Northern minority out for plunder and power.

Jefferson's idea of equality and freedom took in the generations. He abhorred government spending, borrowing, and debt, once suggesting a Constitutional amendment forbidding the U.S. government from borrowing. He writes: "...we must not let our rulers load us with perpetual debt. We must make our election between economy and liberty, or profusion and servitude." Government spending and debt will lead to taxation. If that happens we will "have no time to think, no means of calling the mismanagers to account...private fortunes are destroyed by public as well as by private extravagance. And this is the tendency of all human governments. Public debt is the frightful forerunner. Taxation follows that and in its train wretchedness and oppression." Jefferson in his wildest nightmares could not have foreseen a debt which exceeds the national income, cannot be paid off for untold generations into the future, and much of which is owed to Asian governments.

A very basic idea with Jefferson, stated many times in various forms, is that "the earth belongs in usufruct to the living." Or as he put it another time: "Can one generation bind another, and all others, in succession forever? I think not. The Creator has made the earth for the living...." Here he makes a seeming departure from a conservative respect for tradition and continuity. A living generation need not be bound by the dead hand of the past. Each generation should have just as much freedom to act as did any previous generation, or else freedom becomes a dead thing. The present generation may enjoy the produce of the earth in their time, but they have no right to use up the bounty of the earth that belongs to succeeding generations. If the current generation incurs and passes on heavy debts, then it has committed a deeply immoral act of spending the wealth of future generations for its own benefit. This, I would say is a conservative stand.

Jefferson's informality reveals an important thing about the South and the conflict between North and South that runs through American history. The South was led by genuine aristocrats with a pre-political identity and the North by people whose identity depended on money and office. Is it not relevant that during the War to Prevent Southern Independence, Northern generals, even minor ones, wore glorious uniforms, rode around with large staffs and an entire cavalry squadron as escort, and always commandeered the best available accommodations? General Lee fought the war with one tent, two horses, two aides, a cook, and some messengers, and wore an old colonel's jacket. A British observer who dined at the headquarters mess of Confederate army commander Joe Johnston, which was usually held around a campfire, found that there was only one fork, which the officers took turns in using. This contrast is worth remembering when you hear historians blabber on about a South dominated by a few wealthy slaveholders in contrast to an ideally democratic North.

This suggests a lesson that is worth learning in the study of American history or any history. Superficial and dishonest historians introduce artificial divides and destroy continuity. The primary American mythology tells us that the Founding Fathers made an eternal Union, and, as one of the idiotic Republican presidential hopefuls recently claimed, "worked tirelessly" to eliminate slavery. Later, Southerners, led by Calhoun, invented state rights in their desire to perpetuate slavery forever, repudiated true American principles, and wickedly rebelled against the sacred Union of the Founding Fathers. Note that Confederate generals Lee and Johnston, who I mentioned, were the sons of actual soldiers in the American Revolution, as was President Jefferson Davis. General Lee, as well, had two uncles who signed the Declaration of Independence.

Calhoun's father voted on the original ratification of the Constitution. Thomas Jefferson's grandson served in the Confederate army and government. I could cite hundreds of such facts. Perhaps the most telling is the grandson of Francis Scott Key, author of "The Star Spangled Banner," who was imprisoned as a Southern sympathizer in the same fort about which his grandfather had written the national anthem. He described his jailer, Lincoln, as a brutal tyrant.

My point here is to recognise the continuity in Jeffersonian history. To ignore this continuity is one of the major ways in which our understanding is deceived, and it has been applied pervasively throughout the whole four-century span of American history and culture.

Jefferson was competent in the law like many of his class, but like other Southern leaders, for instance Calhoun, he did not rely on the law for his living or his place in society. This is a significant point. Unlike the major leaders of the North, he never let legalistic thinking or the opinions of judges dominate his view of the Constitution or political society.

Jeffersonian Constitutionalism died long ago, but we need to clarify its relation to later "conservative" theories. Jeffersonians' view of the Constitution was historical. They did not rely on "strict construction" or a judicial idea of "original intent" as is often thought. The language and history of the Constitution was plain. It belonged to the people. The issue is not construction but who is doing the construing.

The people did not need lawyers and judges to tell them what the Constitution meant. Lawyers brought confusion and distortion of plain facts. They argued for pay and for advantage rather than truth. The Constitution in the larger sense was not a legal matter, it was a historical agreement. John Taylor described at length and amusingly how the judges used verbal twisting to justify federal powers that had never been granted. For Jeffersonians the federal courts had progressively undermined free society and the people's will. Jefferson referred to federal judges as "sappers and miners."

Later conservatives like the Federalist Society miss this point and seen to be ignorant of State rights. Their "original intent" reflects the utterly unofficial and unbinding ideas of *The Federalist* and Marshall's early decisions. The Constitutional view thus becomes both legalistic and at the same time subject to vague abstract notions of good government.

John Adams and many others praised the idea of "checks and balances," an idea still touted as meritorious. A strong independent executive, an independent judiciary, and a two-house legislative chamber supposedly provided restraints on dubious actions.

John Taylor made short work of such nonsense. Adams was constructing imaginary orders of society that had no American reality. Checks and balances has been a catastrophic failure. Why should interchangeable politicians in different branches of the federal government check each other? It is in their interest to collaborate to increase federal power. Such a system does not check the federal government, it only allows the government to check the people and States.

St. George Tucker made Jeffersonian Constitutionalism clear in his *A View of the Constitution of the United States* (1803) and his *Commentaries on the Laws of England*, which Americanised and republicanised Blackstone. These were handbooks in the education of lawyers for several generations, more persuasive and perhaps more acceptable to more people than the decisions of Marshall and Story.

For Jefferson it was all clear and simple. We find him declaring to a French scholar, three years after he left the White House,

> But the true barriers of our liberty in this country are our State governments; and the wisest conservative power ever contrived by man, is that of which our Revolution and present government found us possessed. Seventeen distinct States, amalgamated into one as to their, foreign concerns, but single and independent as to their internal Administration.

My intention here has been to understand what Jefferson sees as the good regime. It is a regime where the majority rules while maintaining a healthy suspicion of those who hold power and a willingness to put them in their place. And in the particular American situation this means that the people can and should curtail the central government by acting through the seat of their sovereignty, the States. That, I submit, is the real Jeffersonian democracy. And that understanding characterises Southern thought from Bacon's Rebellion in the 17th century until quite recent times.

8.

THOMAS JEFFERSON: NEW WORLD PHILOSOPHER

*"There is not a truth existing which I fear
or would wish unknown to the whole world."*
—Thomas Jefferson

THE FACT THAT HE WAS THE THIRD PRESIDENT of the United States is not the most important thing, nor, I think, the most interesting thing about Thomas Jefferson, judgment with which he himself agreed. His writings and lifetime corpus of private letters would be one of the richest cultural legacies of his time even if he had never held public office. They cover well over a half century of an active, multi-faceted, and poised genius participating in great events and pursuing an understanding of the world.

Collectors of quotations can easily find several hundred memorable Jefferson observations about government, knowledge, and life. No other President, indeed few political leaders in all of history, can match Jefferson's benevolent and far ranging wisdom.

Today people are considered important if they run for President. Our environment is full of presidential wannabes who have no claim to attention except their own ambitions and publicity. In Jefferson's time, the noble early days of the Union, the assumption was different. Jefferson was not important because he was a President: he was President because he was an important man, because at a critical time he represented the views of and was trusted by a majority of citizens of a majority of the several States. He continued for several subsequent generations to be the chief guide and inspiration for large numbers of Americans.

It is relevant here to note that Jefferson himself, unlike later commentators, knew that there was a distinction between Thomas Jefferson, the renowned philosopher, who discussed ideas in an international correspondence with other great thinkers, and Mr. Jefferson, the public man who led a consensus of Americans as to their government. The public man knew that he was a spokesman and consensus builder for an existing society, not a designer of utopian schemes to be imposed upon it.

In his correspondence with John Adams, Jefferson said the best government was that which provides the most effectually for a pure selection of these natural aristo into the offices of government.

Jefferson's plan for public education in Virginia was a product of this belief. The rich would always take care of the education of their offspring. The public system, where students were culled at every level according to ability, was designed to ensure that talent born into the lower levels of society was not lost to the service of the commonwealth. This is a far cry from the basis of the American public school system which now prevails. That began in Massachusetts when Horace Mann established Prussian style schools, the purpose of which was to make the surly poor and rowdy Catholic immigrants into docile workers.

Jefferson was a product of the New World, of a Virginia society with several generations in America, but was also, as has often been noted, a member of the Enlightenment. North America provided a wonderful variety of new discoveries in the natural world and human arrangements that broadened knowledge. Being free of the complications of the Old World, it also offered opportunities for improvement of human society. For much of his life, until his later years, Jefferson was hopeful of those improvements.

He was always skeptical that the Old World could achieve the opportunities offered by the New World. Several times he referred to the Atlantic Ocean as a blessing separating the New World from the Old. He thought of America as the existing people, with a few rare spirits brought from abroad.

Jefferson learned the ancient Anglo-Saxon language as an aid to understanding the origins of British liberty. He studied the natural world of North America for the advancement of knowledge. He studied American Indian languages and customs because he wanted to understand the brave New World that was the seat of the American experiment in freedom. He was a self-taught architect, designing the Virginia (later Confederate) capitol after a Roman building he saw in France.

Paradoxically to some, Jefferson could not have been the philosopher of the New World had he not been classically educated. It is said that he usually read Greek in the morning. The classics gave him the indispensable knowledge of Western life and history that allowed him to put the New World in comparative perspective. He would likely say that the loss of that perspective is a danger to liberty. He might have approved a bit of utilitarian education but never would have approved the loss of classical education.

For the American Founders, Greece and Rome presented the principles of republican self-government and the examples of unselfish patriotism and sacrifice for the commonwealth. That the Founders did not understand the ancient history accurately, as some claim, does not matter. What is important is what they found in it.

As Jefferson said, the tree of liberty must be watered from time to time by the blood of tyrants and patriots. Those patriots as well as worthy leaders in quieter times needed the proper education. The schooling of future republican leaders was the purpose of Jefferson's curriculum for the University of Virginia.

In 1785, Jefferson took time in Paris to write a long letter of advice to a beloved nephew, Peter Carr, who was about to enter William and Mary College. This missive tells us much about the mind of Jefferson. First, there is an emphasis on truthfulness and honourable behaviour, the same as was given by another Virginian, R.E. Lee, to his sons more than half a century later.

Jefferson hopes to develop a worthy republican leader. He writes of knowledge:

> I can assure you, that the possession of it (next to an honest heart) will above all things render you dear to your friends, and give you fame and promotion in your own country. When your mind shall be well improved with science, nothing will be necessary to place you in the highest points of view, but to pursue the interests of your country, the interests of your friends, and your own interests also, with the purest integrity, the most chaste honour.

There follows a long list of reading requirements—a catalog of 24 Greek and Roman authors of philosophy, history, and literature. These were to be read in the original, not in translation, which seems to tell us Peter, at age 15, was already capable of the classical languages. The list of authors would be daunting to any of today's professors of classics.

This was to be followed by selected modern history, Milton, Shakespeare, Swift, and Pope, the latter two for absorbing good style. More ancient classics, and then natural science. Interestingly, Jefferson remarks:

> You are now, I expect, learning French. You must push this; because the books that will be put into your hands when you advance into Mathematics,

> Natural philosophy, Natural history, etc., will mostly
> be French, these sciences being better treated by the
> French than the English writers.

Jefferson took account that half the New World was Spanish: "Our future connection with Spain renders that the most necessary of the modern languages, after the French. When you become a public man, you may have occasion for it."

Jefferson offered the old truism that a healthy mind requires a healthy body. A day of study should include at least two hours of exercise. His advice in this regard is rather alien to 21st century America:

> As to the species of exercise, I advise the gun. While
> this gives a moderate exercise to the body, it gives
> boldness, independence, and enterprise to the
> mind. Games played with the ball, and others of that
> nature, are too violent for the body, and stamp no
> character on the mind. Let your gun, therefore, be
> the constant companion of your walks.

There is the question of Jefferson's religion. The Christian orthodoxy which has so strongly marked the South grew in power after Jefferson had passed from the scene and was less evident, though certainly not absent, in the colonial and Revolutionary years. It seems fair to say that Jefferson, like many others of his time, tended toward deism. One judges that he believed in a Creator, an Author of our Being, and in Christian moral teachings, but tended to be doubtful about the supernatural aspects of Scripture.

His attitude was quiet and his family remained within the church. He made for himself an abbreviated New Testament that concentrated on the ethical rather than the divine, although, unlike Lincoln, he never wrote anything arrogantly ridiculing Christianity. One can still find diehard Calvinists who dismiss

Jefferson as an atheist. For some reason, critics of Jefferson on such grounds never mention that John Adams and other New Englanders became Unitarians. (Interestingly, Calhoun's religious belief and behaviour resembled Jefferson's.)

Jefferson felt that the organised church historically had been responsible for much superstition that had obscured reason. He considered one of his proudest achievements to be the disestablishment of the Episcopal church in Virginia. This was not really very radical since most of the population was already in other organised Protestant bodies and denominational pluralism and tolerance could hardly be avoided in the American reality.

Then there is Jefferson's famous letter about the "wall of separation" between church and state. The letter was written to a group of Baptists in Connecticut which still had a tax-supported Puritan church. This personal letter has been treated deceitfully by Supreme Court justices and other high persons as if it is a part of the Constitution or even as the characteristic opinion of the Founding Fathers. They omit the decisive part of the letter:

> I consider the government of the United States as interdicted by the Constitution from inter-meddling in religious institutions, their doctrines, discipline, or exercises. This results not only from the provision that no law shall be made respecting the establishment or free exercise of religion, but from that also which reserves to the States the powers not delegated to the United States. Certainly, no power to prescribe any religious exercise, or to assume authority in religious discipline, has been delegated to the General Government. It must, then, rest with the States, so far as it can be in any human authority.

Jefferson's opinion was clearly expressed and is mainstream and exactly what should be expected from an American public man.

JEFFERSONIANS

9.

JOHN TAYLOR OF CAROLINE:
THOMAS JEFFERSON AT HOME

TO EXPLORE THE WRITINGS OF JOHN TAYLOR is, for a 21st century American, an adventure like time travel or visiting a foreign country. It takes some time and effort to understand what is going on, but you return home with a greatly expanded perspective. You will acquire much forgotten wisdom in regard to such matters as constitutional government and political economy, which are of considerable value in an era of judicial activism and billion-dollar bank bailouts.

Thomas Jefferson testified in regard to his fellow Virginia planter and republican: "Col. Taylor and myself have rarely, if ever, differed in any political principle of importance. Every act of his life, and every word he ever wrote, satisfies me of this." It follows that anyone who wants to understand Thomas Jefferson's beliefs and what "Jeffersonian democracy" stood for, should pay attention to the words that John Taylor wrote. Taylor was the systematic expositor of the political position that Jefferson represented in the public mind of his time and for several subsequent generations. In the public mind Jefferson was not the philosophe celebrated or deplored by some later commentators, but the wise republican statesman who put the people before would-be elites and who had defeated the schemes of Alexander Hamilton, John Adams, and their friends to concentrate too much power in the federal government. For his time and long after, Jefferson was less celebrated as the author of "all men are created equal," than as the author of "the principles of 1798," the Kentucky resolutions which had unequivocally declared the right of the sovereign people of a State to counter infringements of the Constitution by the federal government.

Jefferson's name has been invoked to endorse many different ideas and movements. As with any revered figure in history, there are always those who want their agenda to be blessed by postmortem sponsorship. Jefferson lends himself to various uses because he was a cosmopolitan man of letters whose writings would be a treasure of his times even if he had never led a political movement. But as a public man he understood that he was a representative of his society, not a philosopher whose speculations were to be enforced as divine wisdom. Also, he was a leader who needed to maintain a firm national majority and sometimes stated his principles in broad and conciliatory terms.

The real Jefferson emerges for anyone who will read his political papers and letters with an open mind free of assumptions loaded on by later times. This real Jefferson was in sync with John Taylor, as he said. He opposed all unnecessary federal laws, taxes, expenditures, and debt; believed that the sovereignty of the people was to be expressed through their States and that the federal government possessed no sovereignty at all; deplored artificial privileges but believed in an aristocracy of talent; and thought slavery to be an unfortunate problem, while strongly resenting any federal and Northern interference in the matter. Such was the Jeffersonian persuasion, the principles of which were laid out systematically and in depth by John Taylor of Caroline County, Virginia.

We can appreciate the deep conservatism of the Jeffersonian persuasion if we understand Russell Kirk's observation in *The Conservative Mind* that sometimes in telling American history "the acquisitive instinct" has been mistaken for "the conservative disposition."

"Truly conservative statesmen," wrote Kirk, are "leaders whose chief desire is the preservation of the ancient values of society." Jeffersonians sought preservation of what to them was a largely satisfactory American society that had emerged from the colonial experience and the War of Independence, that indeed embodied some ancient British liberties that had been forgotten in the Mother Country. They opposed innovators and devotees of forced "progress," among whom Kirk cites Alexander Hamilton as a conspicuous example. In particular, Jeffersonians feared and opposed innovations that they believed would reconstruct society by putting the government in the service of "the acquisitive instinct." Innovations initiated by Hamilton, which would be revived again in the agendas of the Whig and Republican parties. This opposition was the bedrock political program of Jeffersonian democracy which Taylor in his writings crafted into a persuasive vision of truth and justice.

John Taylor was born in 1753 and died in 1824 at his plantation on the Rappahanock River between Richmond and Fredericksburg. Like Jefferson, Taylor's father died when he was young but left him a sizeable inheritance of land and bonded Africans. Like Jefferson he enjoyed the benefit of gifted mentors—in his case his uncle Edmund Pendleton, prominent among the Revolutionary leaders of Virginia. Like Jefferson, Taylor was educated at the College of William and Mary. Unlike the somewhat older Jefferson, Taylor came of age at the outbreak of the War of Independence and saw much active military duty, characteristically refusing to accept pay and bounties for his patriotic service. He married a daughter of John Penn, a Signer of the Declaration of Independence for North Carolina.

On three different occasions the Virginia General Assembly elected Taylor to fill out terms in the U.S. Senate, quite a compliment for one who did not seek and did not want office and in a state overflowing with talented statesmen. He left aside political office and a lucrative law practice to be a farmer, dedicated to improving the art and science of husbandry for those living on the land, whose interests he defended. For Taylor, a good farmer was more valuable to his fellow citizens than any number of politicians, judges, bankers, stock speculators, or military heroes.

Taylor's wisdom is contained in his books: *A Defense of the Measures of the Administration of Thomas Jefferson* (1804); *Arator: Being a Series of Agricultural Essays, Practical and Political* (1813); *Construction Construed, and Constitutions Vindicated* (1820); *Tyranny Unmasked* (1822); *New Views of the Constitution of the United States* (1823); and *An Inquiry into the Principles and Policy of the Government of the United States* (1814). The last, according to the magisterial American historian Charles A. Beard, "deserves to rank among the two or three really historic contributions to political science which have been produced in the United States."

Taylor's writing style has often been cited as an obstacle to his influence. His friend John Randolph of Roanoke reportedly said that Taylor's books would do much good if they could be translated into English. The criticism is a bit exaggerated. The style is conversational, that of a leisurely eighteenth century essayist or a farmer talking with his neighbours on the verandah. He communicates his understanding as one gentleman to another, with a good deal of humour and satire. Indeed, humour is an effective way to confront the earnest political pundits and disingenuous centralisers of power that have motivated him to write. Referring to the advocates of a strong centralised government, Taylor wrote: "A crocodile has been worshiped, and its priesthood have asserted, that morality required the people to suffer themselves to be eaten by the crocodile." He is not an intellectual historian displaying his learning (which John Adams often seems). Rather than citing obscure bits of history or learned treatises, he refers to Don Quixote. If Sancho Panza had known about government bonds, he would have chosen them as his reward rather than the governorship of an island. Taylor's work belongs in Southern literature as well as political thought.

As the Constitutional scholar James McClellan has pointed out, Taylor's writings are a treasury of golden nuggets. Like this one, which is highly relevant to a time of almost immeasurably vast government debt:

> But an opinion that it is possible, for the present generation to seize and use the property of future generations, has produced to both the parties concerned, effects of the same complexion with the usual fruits of national errour [sic]. The present age is cajoled to tax and enslave itself, by the errour of believing that it taxes and enslaves future ages to enrich itself.

A few other examples of homely political wisdom: "Inferior agents in all wicked plots suffer punishment in this world, whilst their leaders often avoid it until the next." "A power in a government of any form, to deal out wealth and poverty by law, overturns liberty universally; because it is a power by which a nation is infallibly corrupted." "A legislative power of regulating wealth and poverty is a principle of such irresistible tendency, as to bring all political parties to the same standard."

Alexander Hamilton had made the preposterous assertion that "a public debt is a public blessing." It was its very corruption that gave the British government its stability, power, wealth and energy. Meaning that the public debt kept the rich and powerful united with the government by their stake in its interest-bearing bonds, and the availability of wealth gave the ministry ability to command obedient execution of its goals by the bestowal of patronage.

John Taylor was having none of this "paper and patronage aristocracy." Was this not what the War of Independence had been fought to break free of? Who was to pay for this but those who produced the real wealth of the country from the land, and who would become as burdened with taxes as the suffering masses of the Old World? And who was to profit except clever manipulators who produced nothing except paper and persiflage about the allegedly arcane mysteries of finance? Why indeed did the government, which had ample revenue from customs and public land sales, need to borrow at all except to enrich the well-placed at no risk or effort to themselves? A closely related part of the Hamiltonian program was yet another swindle in the eyes of Jeffersonians: the National Bank perverted the Congress's constitutional duty to "regulate the currency" to give private parties the immensely profitable power to create money out of the air by printing paper.

Would not the people, by creating a stronger central authority, be paying for their own chains? And where did the Hamiltonians get the authority for their schemes? Virginia had agreed to no such thing when ratifying a written Constitution creating a government of specifically enumerated, limited, delegated powers. The Philadelphia Convention had voted down a proposal to give the Congress power to create corporations. Yet here was Hamilton arguing that it could do so because such a bank was "necessary and proper" in pursuit of delegated powers. In addition to exposing the bad policy involved, Taylor wrote of the Constitutional issue:

> To me this new notion of a constitution by implication is, I confess, exactly like no Constitution at all; nor has it been proved to my satisfaction, that principles ought to be lost in verbal definitions. [Incorporating the Bank proposes] that an absolute sovereignty as to means does exist, where there is no sovereignty at all as to ends.

[Such a doctrine is] evidently inconsistent with the principle of dividing, limiting, balancing, and restraining political powers.

The habit of corrupting our political system by the instrumentality of inference, convenience and necessity, with an endless series of consequences attached to them, is the importer of contraband principles, and the bountiful grantor of powers not given, or withheld by our constitutions.

Elsewhere, Taylor refers to the drawing of "inferences" from plain language as "alchemy," "superstition," and "witchcraft."

"Political words," he writes, "of all others are the most indefinite, on account of the constant struggle of power to enlarge itself" by ambiguous construction of terms. A "plalanx of words" was being used by the Supreme Court to "distort the plainest provisions of the federal constitution."

All the Founders believed in republican government—a government resting on the consent of the people. Most also understood that such governments suffered from various defects that historically had almost always led to their downfall. The division between Jeffersonian conservatives and their opponents is to some extent represented by differing assessments of the source of danger. Jeffersonians feared "consolidation"—overweening and irresponsible power; the Federalists feared "disunion"—the loss of order, security, and prestige.

Hamilton had said that the people were a great beast—that human nature was flawed, that men were selfish and unreasonable and needed to be managed by their betters. Jefferson immediately had an irrefutable answer. "Where do these angels come from?" If men are flawed, where do you find these superior beings that are entitled to rule others? The remedy for human fallibility was not to empower some but to make sure that power was as divided, limited, temporary, and as directly responsible to the people as possible.

Taylor's *Inquiry* is a reply to John Adams's *Defense of the Constitutions of the United States*. Adams shared the common European and Federalist assumption that unchecked majority rule would inevitably destroy society as the poor majority learned they could vote themselves the wealth of the rich minority. To his credit, Adams also recognised a different though related danger. The rich, powerful, well-born, talented, and glamourous also posed a threat to the commonwealth through their ambitions and self-promotion—too often free governments had ended in the despotic rule of one man. Adams thought that Americans had invented the perfect cure for all these ills. The bicameral legislature, independent judiciary, and executive veto would guard again an unruly majority overstepping its rights. And the distinction and power of the upper house of the legislative body would contain and satisfy the ambitious who might otherwise undermine the state.

Again, Taylor was having none of it. Adams was creating artificial and useless political orders where they did not naturally exist. Such imagined "checks and balances" were no safeguard against the abuses of power. The obvious guard against usurpation of power was to divide and limit it as much as possible, which the American constitutions had done—by providing written specific limits to the role of government in all of its branches. What was most to be guarded against was incremental stretching of those powers. Such stretching alone could legitimate the Hamiltonian program.

Further, wrote Taylor, John Adams was mistaken in his history. Good governments were not normally destroyed by the majority preying upon the wealth of the minority. For Taylor the lesson of history was the opposite. The guileless, unorganised majority of citizens went quietly about the business of earning their bread. They were not the perpetrators but the victims of bad government. The great mass of Europeans were impoverished by the exactions of their rulers, who held power over them for the benefit of a few. But the American population, providentially, was one of independent landowners, along with the merchants, artisans, and professional men who helped sustain agricultural society. The people had property and earnings to protect as well as the rich, and their greatest threat came from the government.

Governments became oppressive when a crafty minority managed to impose itself upon and live off the body of the society. In earlier times this had been done by force and superstition. Now it was to be done by fraud and mystification around words: like "full faith and credit," "necessary and proper," "regulating the currency," and "protecting domestic industry." In Taylor's view:

> The useful and major part of mankind, comprised within natural interests (by which I mean agricultural, commercial, mechanical, and scientific; in opposition to legal and artificial, such as hierarchical, patrician, and banking) is exclusively the object of imposition, whenever words are converted into traitors to principles.

For Taylor, the important conflict was not between the rich and the poor but between the taxpayers and the tax consumers. This long remained for American critics of Hamiltonian government a basic way of understanding politics. The idea still has potency. When Jeffersonians condemned "aristocrats" they meant people with artificial, unearned, government-granted privileges, not talented and honourable men who were the natural and necessary leaders of their communities.

John Adams or John Taylor? Who is the better historian, prophet, and guide?

To recover the Constitution as John Taylor understood and described it requires painstaking intellectual archeology. There is an astounding difference between that basic document and what we have now. Time, ambition, interest, ignorance, deception, misunderstanding, and the lust for power have covered it with layer upon layer of false assumptions and distorted postures.

The Constitution contains no reference to "nation" or "national." Indeed, Taylor observes that the emotional effect and un-reflected associations of "nation" were a major source of Constitutional usurpations and distortions. Throughout the Constitution, "United States" is plural rather than the odd singular it later became. This plural was used in every law, treaty, proclamation, and public discussion from the beginning until well after Taylor's time. Americans sometimes spoke of the "nation" in recognition of a common identity, but their political connection was usually referred to as "the Union," i.e., the Union of the States.

The Declaration of Independence asserts that the thirteen colonies are and of right ought to be independent States. The Constitution announces itself to be "FOR the United States of America," not the "Constitution OF the U.S." or the "U.S. Constitution." With this in mind, read the preamble which declares its purpose is to "form a more perfect Union" in order to "provide for the common defense" and "promote the general Welfare" (of the people of the States). In Article III, section 3, we learn that "Treason against the United States, shall consist only in levying War against THEM, or in adhering to THEIR enemies."

To understand how Taylor saw the Constitution one must forget the iconic status of *The Federalist*. Those essays were a discussion of the Constitution as proposed, not the Constitution as ratified. They were polemics calculated to allay the fears of citizens of New York of a too centralised and irresponsible government (and not particularly successful arguments since ratification passed New York by the narrowest margin). Further, the authors, at least one of them, were obviously insincere. Immediately after securing ratification Hamilton began to claim for the federal government powers that in *The Federalist* he had assured voters it did not possess. Besides, the political wisdom expressed in the essays were opinions—they were not the will of the people and had no official standing whatsoever.

Taylor's Jeffersonian Constitution was not the proposal examined by *The Federalist* but the one ratified by the people of the States. It was to be interpreted in the light of the reservations stipulated in those ratifications, of the Ten Amendments which had been promised as a condition of ratification and which reiterated the limited nature of the federal power, and of the Virginia and Kentucky resolutions of 1798—1800 which restated the sovereignty of the people of the States shortly before Jefferson and his friends assumed power. James Madison agreed, writing that the meaning of the Constitution is to be sought "not in the opinions or intentions of the body which planned and proposed it, but those in the State conventions where it received all the authority which it possesses."

Then and later it was denied that Jefferson had really endorsed State nullification of federal law such as was adopted by South Carolina in 1832. One can only hold this position by ignoring the plain language of these documents. Jefferson, in his last year, and only two years before John C. Calhoun broached the right of nullification, privately recommended that Virginia should once more nullify federal legislation—the internal improvement expenditures that had stretched the powers to establish post roads and regulate interstate commerce into authority to subsidize private corporations to dig canals and construct roads.

Virginia at the time of the War of Independence had a history of five generations and almost two centuries with its own particular pride, identity, laws, and ways of life. Virginians considered their consent to the Constitution (ratification) as a policy to be decided by and for Virginians (in the same way they regarded slavery). The ratification was an act of the sovereign will of a specific people at a specific historical moment, not some vague passive reception of saintly wisdom bestowed by "Founding Fathers" on an amorphous "people of the United States" who did not exist as a constitution-ratifying authority. The Virginia instrument of ratification stated that the sovereign's consent was not eternal but could be revoked when deemed necessary. Taylor's generation and the next several generations of Southerners understood what their fathers and grandfathers had intended in accepting the Constitution, even while the greatest economic and emotional force of the 19th century—nationalism—was gaining strength.

It is an often stated fallacy that Taylor and those who asserted the State rights position were advocates of "strict construction." Taylor (and John C. Calhoun later) specifically rejected the idea that "strict construction" was a safeguard of the Constitution.

The Constitution was not to be interpreted by judges, whatever their philosophy of "construction." No branch of the federal apparatus could be allowed the final judgment as to the limits of its own power. Thus, the later Borkian notion of "original intent," whereby judges adhere to the interpretations in earlier writings and previous court decisions rather than "adapting" the Constitution to new circumstances is an irrelevant and illegitimate realm for Taylor.

In our day, a "living Constitution" is one in which judges exercise the power to change the fundamental document by interpretation, in accordance with their ideas of changing times. Taylor's Constitution was one in which the people of the States were participants in an ongoing process of working out proper Constitutional interpretation. The Constitution was not a one-time opportunity which ever after bound the people of the States to be passive, obedient recipients of whatever any branch of the federal government handed down. The meaning of the Constitution was to be determined by an active participation of the people of the States rather than by the arbitrary decrees of judges. Now that is a real "living Constitution."

The combination of principles that Taylor represents may seem unfamiliar to 21st century Americans, but it is a very American and long enjoyed widespread acceptance. On the one hand a conservative allegiance to the soil and those who labour in it and a defense of local community and inherited ways; on the other a populist suspicion of government and the maneuvers of capitalists, bureaucrats, and reformers. Taylor's writings are prophetic in portraying the downside of the course of history toward ever greater "consolidation." He foresaw the dominance of rent-seeking in the political process, judicial oligarchy, immense debt and burdensome taxation, unhealthy intrusion of the state into private society, and the concentration of wealth and power into fewer and fewer hands.

10.

Nathaniel Macon: Last of the Romans

NATHANIEL MACON IS AN IMPORTANT Founding Father almost unknown these days. Comparing Macon with the politicians of today gives us a benchmark as to how dreadfully far America has degenerated from the principles on which it was founded.

In his time Macon was widely admired by Americans as the perfect model of a republican statesman. By republican I mean republican with a small r. I definitely do not mean the Republican Party, which, from its very beginning, when it stole the name from better people, right up to this minute, has stood for the exact opposite of what Nathaniel Macon meant by republican government.

When North Carolina had occasion in the early 20th century to pick two figures to represent it in the Statuary Hall in the U.S. Capitol, we chose Zeb Vance and Charles Aycock. At the time it was natural to honour Vance who had seen us through the horrible war of conquest waged against us, and Aycock, who removed the last vestiges of Reconstruction. That's understandable, although it overlooked Macon, who might easily qualify as the greatest Tar Heel of all.

Macon was born in 1758 on a plantation in Warren County, where he lived his entire life. He was a student at what is now Princeton when the War of Independence broke out in 1775. He left school and joined the New Jersey militia on active service, and then went home and joined the North Carolina troops. He was offered but refused a commission and he refused also the bounty that was paid for enlisting. He served in the Southern campaigns until he was elected to the General Assembly near the end of the war while he was still in his 20s. In the next few years he was offered a place in the North Carolina delegation to the Continental Congress which he declined. It is noteworthy that his brother John voted against ratification of the new U.S. the Constitution in both conventions of the sovereign people of North Carolina to consider that question; and that the State did not ratify until the first ten amendments, especially the Ninth and Tenth, were in place to limit the federal government.

As soon as the U.S. government went into operation, Hamilton and his Yankee friends, claiming that they were acting on behalf of "good government," began to turn the government into a centralised power and a money-making machine for themselves by banks, tariffs, government bonds, and other paper swindles that would be paid for out of the pockets of the farmers, who produced the tangible wealth of the country. To oppose this Macon accepted election to the U.S. House of Representatives for the Second Congress. He served in the House 24 years and the Senate 13 years, representing North Carolina in congress from 1791 to 1828, from the age of 33 to the age of 70 when he retired voluntarily. He was Speaker for six years, chairman of the foreign affairs committee in both the House and Senate, and finally President Pro Tem of the Senate. He received numerous overtures to be a candidate for Vice-President and was twice offered appointments to the Cabinet, all of which he turned down. During all this time he never neglected his duties as justice of the peace and militia officer in Warren County. His last public service was to preside over the North Carolina constitutional convention of 1835, and he died two years later. The city of Macon, Georgia, Randolph-Macon College, and counties in Alabama, Tennessee, and Illinois as well as North Carolina were named for him.

During all this time Macon was admired because he never changed from the principles with which he began. What were these principles? The federal government should be tightly bound by the Constitution. It should not tax the people and spend money any more than was absolutely necessary for the things it was entitled to do, nor go into debt, which was just a way to make the taxpayers pay interest to the rich. Eternal vigilance was the price of liberty. Power was always stealing from the many to the few. Officeholders were to be watched closely and kept as directly responsible to the citizens as possible. A few words from Macon in Congress often stopped bills that proposed supposedly attractive measures. It might be nice to pay for everybody to go to college, or to build a fancy temple for the Supreme Court, or to issue bonds for rich people to invest in, or overturn a dictator 5,000 miles away. But the politicians had no right to take away the citizens' earnings for whatever they thought was good. The Constitution told them what they could do.

History showed that the stronger and more centralised a government became the less free were the people. And the richer the government and its politicians and beneficiaries became, the poorer were the people. That was what had always happened, but America, with governments created by the people, had a chance to avoid the bad tendencies of government of the past. As time went on, Macon realised more and more that preserving true republican principles was a losing cause, but in the company of John Randolph and John Taylor he never wavered even when most of his fellow Jeffersonians were willing to yield some ground.

The offices Macon held are not the important thing. Today politicians scramble to get into office so they can have honour and importance as well as make money and flatter their vanity. But Macon, like Washington and Jefferson, was not important and respected because he was elected to office. He was elected to office because he was important and respected. He never campaigned for an office. He never attended a party caucus. He never promised anyone patronage to support him. Macon was elected over and over and revered because of what he was.

John Randolph of Roanoke, literally on his death bed referred to Macon as the wisest man he ever knew. Thomas Jefferson called him "the last of the Romans," and he meant that as a high compliment—that Macon was the model of a selfless patriot and a principled republican. In fact, Macon was more Jeffersonian than Jefferson himself.

The American Founders much admired the heroes of republican Rome which is why George Washington has a statue in a toga— Roman heroes like Cincinnatus, who was plowing his fields when they came to him and said the republic was in peril. He left, took command of the army, defeated the enemy, and then returned to continue plowing his fields. He sought nothing for himself, only to serve his country and maintain its principles. This was the kind of republican hero that Macon represented to Americans. He valued the respect of his countrymen but had no ambition for profit or glory for himself. It was men ambitious for glory and profit who had subverted freedom throughout history.

A negative opinion of Macon was expressed by President John Quincy Adams in his secret diary. He excoriated Macon for being responsible for defeating many of Adams's schemes for a stronger and more meddlesome federal government. Adams, in the typical Yankee way, thought Macon opposed him only because he was not as smart as Adams himself. This even was written in secret at the same time Adams was trying to persuade Macon to be his Vice President.

Good Americans of the Founding and for several generations thereafter praised the idea of "republican simplicity." A free government of the people did not need the fancy costumes and ceremonies of European courts. This is why Jefferson walked to his inauguration in a plain suit, delivered his state of the Union message in writing rather than preaching to the assembled congressmen like a monarch on a throne, and made his White House social events as informal as possible.

Here is something else important to note about early American history. Genuine Southern aristocrats like Jefferson and Macon believed in government responsible to the people. The Northerners, who had no claim to aristocracy, wanted to use the government to aggrandize themselves. President John Adams rode around in a coach with white horses and insisted on being addressed as "Your Excellency." When Macon was living at ease among his 70 slaves, John Adams was fortifying his house in fear that American mobs might attack him like they were doing in France. Of course, Macon, like all the other Jeffersonians, knew without doubt that Northern attacks on slavery were malicious, counter-productive, and driven by lust for power rather than benevolence.

Here is another interesting fact about the North and the South that never gets into the history books. The history of the Revolution is written as if those who were fighting it were striving to achieve a strong central government for Americans. This is a lie promoted during the 19th century. It was true of some Revolutionary soldiers like Hamilton and Marshall. But it was not true of John Taylor, James Monroe, and St. George Tucker of Virginia, Nathaniel Macon of North Carolina, Thomas Sumter and Andrew Pickens of South Carolina, or James Jackson of Georgia. These and many others had fought the Revolution to get out from under a government that was levying taxes and sending troops and bureaucrats to restrict the liberty and prey on the property of Americans. They did not want to establish a government that had too much power and was too remote from the people, even if it was an American government. And, while New Englanders who had served three inactive months in the militia lined up to claim federal pensions for Revolutionary War service, the Southerners refused to accept money taxed from the people for doing their duty.

Government had to be kept as close to the people as possible. Macon's North Carolina in the beginning elected General Assembly anew each year, and the General Assembly chose the governor for a one-year term. Macon opposed the change to longer terms in the constitutional revision of 1835. You can imagine what he thought about U.S. Senators serving six years and federal judges serving for life. These were no longer responsible to the people. Officials had to be known to the people and reviewed frequently to make sure they were behaving and not exceeding their powers. Politics should not be a profession. Politicians should make their own living just like everyone else. They were just citizens performing temporarily a service who would soon return to private life and live under the laws they had made.

Macon owned much land and many slaves and was a national hero. Yet he lived very simply in a rather remote location—so remote that I confess I once spent half a day driving around Warren County with three different sets of directions and never found it. He attended the Baptist Church accompanied by his slaves. He was buried very unostentatiously. As far as I can find, only one portrait was ever painted of him, the one that was customarily made of Speakers of the House.

Nathaniel Macon summed up his philosophy in advice to a young Tar Heel: "Remember, you belong to a meek state and a just people, who want nothing but to enjoy the fruits of their labour honestly and lay out the profits in their own way."

By the end of his life Macon had realised that the cause of republicanism was lost at the federal level, and also that the North was determined to exploit and rule the South. South Carolina tried in 1832 to use "nullification," state interposition, to force the federal government back within the limits of the Constitution. After he read Andrew Jackson's proclamation against South Carolina, Macon told friends that it was too late for nullification. The Constitution was dead. The only recourse was secession. There was nothing left but for the South to get out from under the "Union" and govern itself.

Thirty years later, in the spring of 1861, the North Carolina convention met to unanimously ratify secession. Nathaniel Macon's son-in-law, Weldon N. Edwards, was in the president's chair.

Nathaniel Macon left us an invaluable Jeffersonian legacy from which we can learn much about the way things should be.

11.

Little Jemmy's Last Hurrah

Review of *The Last of the Fathers: James Madison
and the Republican Legacy,* by Drew R. McCoy.

JAMES MADISON WAS NOT "The Father of the Constitution."
I know you were probably taught that in school. I myself am guilty
of having foisted that old truism of the history classroom off on
countless sullen but gullible undergraduates.

That comes of my believing what I was told, until firsthand
investigation and reflection taught me better. What Madison is
the father of is every trimming and time-serving politician who
ever played the middle against both ends, obscured the real issues
with verbiage, and bent the Constitution to fit his own abstract
conceptions of government.

All of Madison's prominence was owed to four factors—an over-
facile pen; his family connections; his friendship with Jefferson;
and his staying power (though he considered himself too frail to
take part in the War of Independence in his 20s, he lived to be 85,
being the last surviving member of the Philadelphia Convention
and leaving the most extensive notes of the proceedings of that
closed-door affair).

Far from being the prominent member of the Convention that he portrayed himself to be, having pushed himself in by means of his father's great holdings in one part of Virginia, he found his overly grandiose and overly abstract schemes swiftly shunted aside by more experienced and sensible men. (M.E. Bradford has given a good account of this in "The Great Convention as Comic Action.") His role in securing ratification in Virginia has often been exaggerated, as has the influence, at the time, of *The Federalist Papers*. As if such men as General Washington and John Marshall needed the help of little Jemmy Madison in securing approval of the Constitution!

His election as President rested not on any merit or popularity of his own, but simply on his friendship with Jefferson, by which he managed by a narrow margin to win precedence over Monroe, a far better man though not as artful a dodger. Madison left the Presidency having failed as an executive, as a party leader, and as a national symbol. His large reputation in history is mostly a creation of much later times—the New Deal era—especially when politicians have found his ambiguous and protean Constitution amenable to their purposes.

Madison was not in any sense a great thinker. In Jefferson's letters and writings, we can find hundreds of quotable and striking thoughts; in all of Madison's vast scribblings, very little. Of all the Founding Fathers, he, because of his superficiality, lends himself the most readily to modernization and liberalization. That is why he is called "The Father of the Constitution."

Throughout his life, as is amply documented here, though to a different import than I am placing on it, he did all in his power to prevent issues from being clarified and settled, which is the classic attitude of the politician as opposed to the statesman. First allied with Hamilton in the attempt to secure a strongly centralized government, he shifted to an alliance with Jefferson to the opposite end. In his later years, which are covered by this book, during the nullification crisis he played both sides for all they were worth. First, he denied that the interposition of South

Carolina against the tariff was the same thing as had been initiated (if not consummated) by Virginia and Kentucky in 1798–99, which was a falsehood. In response, Jefferson's son-in-law produced the original draft of the Kentucky Resolutions in Jefferson's hand, which was an even stronger assertion of state sovereignty than what was actually adopted. Madison attacked nullification for going too far, and then he attacked its opponents for going too far the other way. This might be considered, as it is by Professor McCoy, to be a noble pursuit of "balance" among viewpoints. It might also be considered lying and cowardice.

There were in the early Republic only two honest positions to take. One was to side with Hamilton, Marshall, and Webster in the pursuit of a vigorous centralized government. The other choice was to follow Jefferson, John Taylor, and Calhoun in defending the agrarian republic. Congressional sovereignty versus state sovereignty; a commercial progressive society versus an agrarian one. There was no question that the overwhelming majority of people preferred the Jeffersonian version at first, if not later. Both these positions were forthright and patriotic, involving a sincere vision of the future of America.

Madison's response—exactly that of the vile cunning politician and the timid scholar in any situation—was to take both positions at once: divided sovereignty, whatever that is, and a "balance" of interests. He was followed in this by a host of cunning politicians, especially Martin Van Buren, the real architect of modern American democracy (and not his unwitting cover, Andrew Jackson). The practical result was to confuse the issues hopelessly, to prevent their clarification and peaceful solution, and to render the national discourse forever into a deceitful game that avoided real issues.

Since Madison's later career was spent on the Jeffersonian side, he did the most extensive damage to that side—by professing to uphold its principles while constantly cutting the ground from under them. His role in the slavery controversy was the same. He condemned slavery in principle, and also condemned its opposite, antislavery.

I should make it clear that I am conveying my view of Madison, not Professor McCoy's. He is a good deal more scholarly, sympathetic, and temperate in his evaluation than I am, though he is certainly aware of, and explores in detail and with insight, some of the ambiguities I have mentioned.

This book deals with Madison's later years (he left the White House in 1817 and lived until 1836) and with certain of his disciples of the next generation, whose careers and ideas are traced up to the Civil War and beyond. Thus, the book is not about the early Republic, but is a study of antebellum America and particularly of the slavery issue, which Madison and his heirs failed totally to cope with. This middle period of American history is in many ways the most important and the least understood part of our past, and this book is an honest, original, and penetrating look at some aspects of it.

One of the most interesting unasked questions in American history is what happened to Virginia after its central and premier role in the Revolution and the early Republic. It retained for a long time its prestige, and any significant Virginia politician was ipso facto a national figure, but after Monroe it failed to make any creative or even important contribution to our political history. This was something that Calhoun often pointed out: If Virginia would only get its act together and take its proper place at the head of the Union, most problems could be solved. McCoy does not answer the question "why not" fully, but he asks it and contributes to its answer.

There are several reasons why most American historians have not asked the question. One is that they lack sufficient historical imagination for it to have occurred to them. A more important reason is that modern Americans are simply emotionally incapable of recognizing the fact that a preponderance of their great Founders and early leaders were, in their primary social identity, Southern slaveholders. Thus, they are condemned always to puerile and superficial misunderstandings of their own history. For some reason it is easier to put this fact out of mind in dealing with the early period than with the antebellum period, although, in fact, slavery was quite as salient in American life in 1787, if not more so, as in 1860. McCoy is too good a historian to avoid the hard issues, however.

Madison spent his entire life as a slaveholder, and a major one, although like Jefferson and some others—though not all of the Southern leaders of the early Republic—he was theoretically opposed to it. He was never able, and McCoy suggests, not really willing, to do anything about it, which, obviously, was a great tragedy. Much of the book is concerned with three followers of Madison in the next generation who also failed to make much headway: Edward Coles, Nicholas P. Trist, and William Cabell Rives. Thus, we have an intimate firsthand view of the Madisonian legacy in the immediate post-Madisonian period.

All three of these figures were Virginians of the planter class. Coles moved to Illinois, emancipated his slaves, and played an important part in averting the real possibility of slavery being introduced legally into Illinois. Thereafter, he became increasingly bitter and marginalized. Having, he thought, attempted to implement the Madisonian desire for emancipation, he found Madison to be, in fact, restraining and rather lukewarm.

Nicholas P. Trist, another emigré Virginian, was an intellectual dilettante who spent most of his life in minor patronage positions in the federal government. He attempted, unsuccessfully, to apply "Madisonian" principles of balance to the seam-splitting, unruly America of the Jacksonian and antebellum eras, but only succeeded in being ineffectual and irrelevant.

The most important, but least interesting, of the three junior Madisonians was Rives, who was off and on Senator from Virginia as well as U.S. Minister to France, Madison's official biographer, and probably as famous a figure in his own time as Calhoun, Clay, or Webster. Rives played the perfect Madisonian role in national politics. He was definitely for state rights, but nullification was going too far. The South was definitely justified in rebutting outside interference with slavery, but it was not justified in actually defending slavery. When the question was national bank or no national bank, Rives supported a sort of semi national bank.

Having spent his entire career working, with considerable success, to disrupt Calhoun's efforts to clarify the issues to their fundamentals and unite the South, he ended—too late by his own standards—in the 1860's exactly where Calhoun had been decades before: as a member of the Confederate Congress. It was a career of total foolishness and failure.

What is most valuable in Professor McCoy's work is his exploration of all the gradations of opinion and reaction of Madison and his three disciples as they attempted to apply their version of the Founding principles to new times and new forces. These were not few and simple views and responses but many and complex ones, as McCoy makes clear in his sophisticated exposition, and they were concerned with such fundamental matters as executive versus legislative power, or state versus central authority; with traditional principles of political economy confronted by new conditions; and with the issue of slavery and the position of the black minority in American society.

The bottom line is an indication of failure. McCoy, like any good modern, sees this failure as a sign of moral weakness in Madison and in men like him who did not follow through on their professed antislavery views by becoming abolitionists and egalitarians. In a sense, this is an unhistorical reading of the period, because freeing the black people was simply not as important a priority to Madison as it now seems to us, nor was it ever conceivable for him to adopt the modern role of Olympian reformer or to forward emancipation without riding roughshod over all the principles of government that he held sacred.

But failure did occur in a way the author does not recognize. When a real leader appeared—Calhoun, who was also a statesman and political thinker of a high order—it was the Madisonian legacy of trimming and seeking an artificial "balance" that prevented the only solution that was possible in Madison's own conception of government: It was for the South to unite itself sufficiently to deal with the issues in its own time and in its own way according to federal and consensual principles within the Union. The failure to do so created, finally, a situation with no issue except conquest and the permanent destruction of the old federal Republic, which had been Madison's fondest hope to preserve.

12.

LITTLE JEMMY RIDES AGAIN

Review of *James Madison and the Making of America* by Kevin R.C. Gutzman

BOOKS THAT REFER IN THEIR TITLES TO "the making of America" should generally be avoided. It is a meaningless phrase except in the realm of nationalistic mysticism. "America" was not made—it grew. It certainly was not "made" by James Madison, who only officiously tinkered with its surface. And which "America" is meant? There have existed a number of different versions. Used in such a way, the term can only mean an imaginary "America" of vague sentimentality which has never really existed.

I wish that Gutzman's book had been simply titled *James Madison: A Biography*, for it is a better work of historianship than its hokey title suggests. Kevin Guzman is one of the abler young historians of the day. He is steeped in the primary sources of the Founding and early national periods, sees things that have been missed by generations of celebrity historians, and writes well, with a light touch. His new biography is being billed as the new standard on its subject. There is justice in this judgment. The work is rich in context and detail, tells us all we will ever really want to know about "Little Jemmy" Madison, and is a moderate and balanced account of the subject and his times. The author understands the

Virginia context, and therefore Madison, better than anyone has in a long time. The book is doubtless also a good career move, raising the author of *The Politically Incorrect Guide to the Constitution* to establishment respectability. In a way that is too bad, because Madison is a waste of his talents.

One of the advance endorsements of the book tells us that Madison is one of the most interesting of the Founders. That is total bosh. Little Jemmy is the least interesting of the Founders. He is a colossal bore. If his father had not been one of the largest land and slave owners in his part of Virginia, we would never have heard of him. A tireless scribbler, his learning and understanding were pedestrian, that of a pedant, and not remotely in a class with Jefferson or John Adams or many others of the Founders. Pedestrian thinkers and pedants have elevated him to "Father of the Constitution" because his writings contribute to a false nationalistic interpretation of the Founding. In fact, Madison, who was of very junior standing among the delegates at Philadelphia, arrived with grandiose plans that were quickly shot down. He lost more votes than he won in the Convention. Pedants and pedestrian thinkers love him for his speculations in *The Federalist*, which was a partisan and disingenuous treatise that was never ratified by the people or anybody else, does not discuss the Constitution that was actually ratified as opposed to the one that was proposed, and has absolutely no legitimate standing for Constitutional interpretation. Madison himself said that the Constitution should be interpreted solely by the state ratifications which alone gave it authority.

Jefferson befriended him and used him as a sounding board, perhaps because he realized that Madison was more in touch with everyday opinion, but it was a sad day when the Democratic Republican caucus narrowly chose Little Jemmy as Jefferson's successor over James Monroe, a far better man. Unlike Madison, Monroe was a man of sound judgment with executive, military, and diplomatic experience. Madison never went abroad and despite the fact that his health in his twenties was allegedly too feeble to allow him to fight in the War of Independence, he lived into his eighties. Most people found him dull company.

He was no great shakes as Secretary of State and as President failed completely in multiple ways. Not until George W. Bush did we have another chief executive so weak and incompetent as to allow foreigners to attack the capital city while he fled to safety. Madison was always jumping back and forth. He encouraged Congress to adopt a plan of internal improvements, and then on his last day in office vetoed it. Having come into prominence opposing the first national bank, he sponsored the second one. A mere thirty years after Jefferson and Madison asserted the right of State interposition against unconstitutional federal acts, he claimed that South Carolina's action against the tariff was not the same thing. This, as Guzman previously has pointed out in a signal article, was a lie. (He puts it a little more politely.)

Madison's political speculations are abstract and invariably have been proved wrong (like the "extended republic," the ludicrous notion of "divided sovereignty," and the argument that the federal judiciary could never pose a problem of usurpation). His thinking is that of a professor rather than a statesman. Second-string "political philosophers" and "constitutional scholars" identify with Madison's scribbling and fancy themselves sharing in Deep Thoughts about government. When read closely, Gutzman's work is actually less worshipful and more realistic than most other treatments of Madison. But then, nowadays who is going to read closely? "Scholars" these days don't read and react to books. They just find out what is fashionable to think about them and repeat it.

JEFFERSON AND THE HISTORIANS

13.

Thomas Jefferson, Conservative

on Dumas Malone's *Jefferson and His Times*

IN 1809 THOMAS JEFFERSON yielded up the Presidency and crossed into Virginia. In the 13 active years remaining to him he never left it. The first volume of Malone's masterpiece, published in 1948, was *Jefferson the Virginian*. The sixth and last is *The Sage of Monticello*. Jefferson begins and ends with Virginia. Keep this fact in mind. It will save us from many errors and lead us as near to the truth as we can get in regard to this sometimes enigmatic Founding Father.

No great American, not even Lincoln, has been put to so many contradictory uses by later generations of enemies and apologists, and therefore none has undergone so much distortion. In fact, most of what has been asserted about Jefferson in the last hundred years—and even more of what has been implied or assumed about him—is so lacking in context and proportion as to be essentially false. What we commonly see is not Jefferson. It is a strange amalgam or composite in which the misconceptions of each succeeding generation have been combined and recombined until the original is no longer discernible.

Presuming we wish to know Jefferson rather than simply to manipulate his image for our own purposes, Malone is indispensable. *Jefferson and His Time* is a conspicuous example of an increasingly rare phenomenon, genuine scholarship. I mean that term as a compliment—to denote a work that avoids the extremes of pedantry and superficiality, that is exhaustive, thorough, honest, balanced, felicitous, reasonable, and executed on a noble scale.

From Malone, and especially from the sixth volume, we can if we wish, begin to discern the real Jefferson. And that Jefferson is in the broad outline of American history, identifiable in no other way than as a conservative. The real Jefferson is most visible in his last years. I do not mean by this that Jefferson was one of those proverbial persons who was liberal in youth and conservative in old age. There is no conflict between the young Jefferson and the old Jefferson except in the perceptions of image-manipulators. Jefferson was of a piece, his main themes were constant. But I do mean that the conservative Jefferson emerged most clearly in the last years, when he was not in office, when he was not bound by the necessary compromises of leading a party or speaking in the voice of community consensus rather than his own voice, when he was down home in his natural environment.

How did we get so far afield that it has taken half the lifetime of a great historian to recover the wherewithal of a proper understanding of Jefferson? First, New Englanders, embittered by the half-century setback which Jefferson and his friends administered after 1800 to their political style and goals, painted him as an effete snob, a visionary, a kind of squeamish Jacobin. If the New England Federalists and their descendants lacked political power, they made up for it in cultural power. Their loss at the polls was turned into a victory in the sophisticated battleground of historical writing. The understanding of Jefferson and his accomplishments that was handed down to posterity was created by Henry Adams. Adams, with brilliance, painstaking care and a cunningly contrived pseudo-objectivity, structured a perception of Jefferson and his times from which American historians—

until Malone—had never really escaped. Jefferson, even when viewed sympathetically, was judged by New England standards. This meant that the essential outlines of his Virginian frame of reference were obliterated. Thus, the mainsprings of his belief and action could not be detected accurately.

Jefferson's admirers have done him little better. It seemed that the Civil War and Federalist historians had repudiated and buried Jefferson forever. Then along came Vernon I. Parrington, the son of an English socialist raised in Kansas, who rediscovered Jefferson the agrarian liberal. But unfortunately, what Parrington discovered was an imaginary combination of French philosophe and midwestern populist, not the planter of Albemarle County. Parrington, Claude Bowers and a host of other worthies soon turned Jefferson into the patron saint of Wilsonism, the New Deal and what passed for "democracy."

Thus, by a strange piling-up of ironies, the intellectual descendants of Jefferson's opponents converted him into one of them, a kind of urban, liberal, puritan dogmatist of egalitarianism. More recently, some of them, like Fawn Brodie, have discovered that the evidence does not fit this image, that Jefferson never was a certifiable modern liberal. They should have admitted that they had been wrong all along. Instead, they chose to brand Jefferson as an aberration and a hypocrite for not being one of them, that is for not being what he never was and never wanted to be. Jefferson was an American republican, not a European social democrat. Jefferson was agrarian, not urban and industrial. Jefferson was a gentleman, which the class of admirers I am talking about here certainly are not.

All of these distorted notions of Jefferson have been possible only because of a lack of context, plausible because they have extrapolated one small portion of Jefferson and built an image on that foundation. This has been most conspicuous in the peculiar, dogmatic, ahistorical rendering of one phrase of the Declaration of Independence as a piece of egalitarian revelation. Indeed, without this one distortion of Jefferson (and of American history) the contemporary American left could hardly be seen to have any legitimate tradition at all. (Even more peculiarly, the same dogma is embraced as a main tenet by one school of "conservative" political scientists.)

There is one other important reason for misreading Jefferson that must be taken into account. Jefferson can be misunderstood in the same way that any great writer is subject to conflicting interpretations. And Jefferson is important as a writer, a thinker and a stylist. If he had never held public office, the immense body of his private correspondence would still be one of the most important American cultural legacies of his period. In his correspondence he was imaginative, playful, speculative. He adapted himself somewhat to the person he was addressing. He liked to turn ideas around and examine them from all angles. Except in his most narrowly political activities he wrote as a philosopher, not as a tactician. Further, he was intellectually polite and magnanimous. Dogmatists found that Jefferson did not contradict them in person. When they later discovered that he disagreed, they called him a hypocrite. He was not: he was simply a polite listener, a gentleman. Thus Jefferson can be quoted against Jefferson. In order to see clearly the real Jefferson we have to know the context, we have to know the whole corpus of work, we have to know which were the constant themes and which the occasional ones. This Malone has made possible.

Who, then, was the real Jefferson? What were these constant themes? They are clear. None offer comfort to the contemporary left. First of all, Jefferson stood for freedom and enlightenment. That he is our best symbol for these virtuous goals is Malone's central theme. That does not mean, however, that his thought can be twisted to support something that very different men with very different goals postulate to be freedom and enlightenment. His concepts of freedom and enlightenment were always rooted in the given nature and the necessities of his Virginia community and always balanced harmoniously against competing claims. Read Jefferson on the need for every citizen to be a soldier, on the prudential limits that should have been observed in the French

Revolution, on the inappropriateness of liberty for a people unprepared for it; read of Jefferson's approval of Governor Patrick Henry's summary execution of a Tory marauder.

Jefferson favored the liberty of the individual and the community, and he had in mind certain reforms that he felt would enhance them. However, Jefferson was nothing if not the enemy of programmatic, government-imposed reforms. His whole career proved this. But read his reaction to the nationalistic program of our first "progressive" President, John Quincy Adams:

> When all government, domestic and foreign, in little as in great things, shall be drawn to Washington as the centre of all power, it will render powerless the checks provided of one government on another, and will become as venal and oppressive as the government from which we have separated.

Jefferson is on record as fearing the harmful effects of slavery on the community. But he feared more the harmful effects of political antislavery. Read him on the Missouri controversy and you will correct a thousand misrepresentations. Jefferson, it is true, wanted America to be an example to all mankind of successful free government. But when he said example that is just what he meant, example. He gives no comfort to those who want to impose democracy on others, but much comfort to those who want to defend American democracy from any and all enemies. Jefferson, it is true, mistrusted the clergy. In this respect he was typical of many in his generation. But Jefferson the citizen, as opposed to Jefferson the philosopher, lived within the church. Religion and piety troubled him not at all. What he feared was the sanctimonious, intermeddling, politicized Calvinist clergy—that is, what we would today call "progressive" churchmen.

Jefferson was the advocate of a free economy, but he was not doctrinaire about it. Like all his values, his belief in the free market was balanced against other claims. He believed in economic freedom within a stable society. Malone's chapter, "The Political Economy of a Country Gentleman," by simple adherence to the facts, corrects four generations of distortion. When viewed "in retrospect," he writes, Jefferson's "reaction to the economic problems of his day can better be described as conservative."

Jefferson championed public education, but it was not public education on the leveling Prussian-New England model that later became the American standard. The traditional classical curriculum was to be supplemented by more modern and practical subjects, but not jettisoned to make room for them. It was to be an education competitive, elitist, based on a belief in a natural aristocracy of talents and virtues. The rich would always take care of themselves. The purpose of public education was to make sure that the talented ones who appeared among the poor would not be lost. That is the exact opposite of what modern American public education aims at, for its goal is to reduce the educational level to the lowest common denominator—which, in effect, guarantees that the poor but promising youth does not learn enough to rise above his station or to compete with the privileged. "The natural aristocracy," wrote Jefferson, "I consider as the most precious gift of nature for the instruction, the trusts and government of society.... May we not even say that the government is best which provides most effectually for a pure selection of these natural aristo into the offices of government?"

Dumas Malone has completed a great work—a work that is, like its subject, truthful, harmonious, balanced, fair, decorous, gentlemanly. What a rare thing for an American book in the 20th century, a book by a gentleman about a gentleman.

14.

THE CONSENSUS JEFFERSON

Review of *In Pursuit of Reason: The Life of*
Thomas Jefferson, by Noble E. Cunningham

WITH THE EXCEPTION OF THE DRIVEN and depressed
Lincoln, no major figure in American history is, in the final analysis,
more enigmatic than Jefferson. Without any exception, none is
more complex. There is more to the enigma and complexity than
a multitude of facets—political leader, botanist, architect, linguist,
ethnographer, musician, man of letters, and much else. (If he
had never held a public office. Jefferson's correspondence would
still be one of the most valuable treasures of his era.) But behind
these varied roles was a mind of a very high order. With deep
and complicated reserves, yet covered by an impenetrable mask
of everyday balance and harmony that was more than sufficient
for the highest worldly success without beginning to exhaust its
capacity or reveal its real nature. In many respects, the enigma
of Jefferson, delightfully hinted at in Albert Jay Nock's early 20th
century biography, is similar to that of his contemporary, Goethe,
and likewise will remain forever inaccessible to those of us who do
not enjoy the mental and moral gifts of nature in such abundance.

But we do not really need to understand the whole personality to grasp the significance of Jefferson's career as a public man in the founding years of the American republic, and this new biography is concerned chiefly with the career of the public man. There was no mystery at all in what Jefferson stood for in the American political scene. This was clearly understood in his time and for a generation or two thereafter by both his friends and his enemies. But, while there is no mystery, there is a great deal of confusion, arising out of subsequent efforts to manipulate his image as an aegis for other causes of other days. Even had he not been so complex a puzzle as a man, his role in American history is so covered by ideological debris that reality can only be uncovered inch by inch. (Merrill D. Peterson's tour de force, *The Jefferson Image in the American Mind*, 1960, showed the many and contradictory uses to which he has been put.) In fact, the multivarious misunderstandings of Jefferson's political career tell us little about him. They tell us a great deal about the fragmentation, shallowness, and image-mongering that characterized American political and intellectual life after his time, a degeneration which he observed in his last years.

Jefferson had a chivalric and optimistic faith that the intelligence and patriotism of his fellow American freeholders (outside of Massachusetts and Connecticut) were such that they could be trusted to rule themselves. It followed that a free republican government was the proper form of government for Americans and that this government should interfere in their private affairs and pick their pockets as little as was consistent with public order and national independence. Unlike persons in the 19th century and since who seized upon and universalized a few words in the Declaration of Independence, he did not insist that liberty and republicanism were appropriate to every people, condition, and time. The element of messianic democratic universalism that came to characterize the American approach to the world was a product of a later time and was a devolved expression of that New England Puritanism which Jefferson despised, and which hated him.

To Jefferson and his friends, his victory and theirs in 1800 meant simply that they had established his view (which was not something he invented and promulgated from on high as a divine lawgiver, but something that arose naturally out of American conditions) as predominant. Yet by the time he died, in John Quincy Adams's would-be activist presidency, Jefferson well knew that his victory had been temporary.

The LSU Press has inaugurated a new series of Southern biographies, of which this is an early entry. The goal is a readable one-volume treatment, based upon accumulated scholarship and reflection, but aimed, apparently, at general readers. Given the alienation between historical scholarship and the reading public (if such a thing still exists), this is laudable. But it is hard to imagine a more difficult subject to take on in this way than Jefferson. There are many good, specialized studies of particular aspects of Jefferson and room for many more, but it is no easy matter to boil him down to one smooth volume. The author sought to bypass all the accretions of confusion and to see Jefferson afresh, while admitting that he presents only his own view of a complicated subject. This is probably the proper strategy for the occasion, but perhaps unavoidably, it can succeed only at the cost of either distortion or blandness, in this case the latter. This is, in a way, a redundant book, though responsibly and gracefully written. Did I desire a readable and up-to-date one-volume life of Jefferson, I would hire the most skilled available editor to condense Dumas Malone's six volumes, which are as close to definitive as history can ever be. The book in hand fills a formal requirement, without adding anything either factual or interpretive to the world's body of knowledge.

Cunningham hoped to see Jefferson afresh and thus sought to reduce his life to a clear and manageable theme, his faith in reason in the affairs of man. Here I must part company with the author. While the observation is true, it is so general as to be nearly meaningless or, what is worse, lends itself to too many misrepresentations. Almost all the errors and confusions about Jefferson result from using his faith in man's reasonableness to provide an endorsement for any later movement which appealed to reason, no matter how different in spirit, in tacit assumptions, in social context, in intellectual fabric from Jefferson's own. Alexander Hamilton also believed in reason, but he drew rather different conclusions about its proper use. One would never gather from Cunningham's mild consensus history that the gentlemen's disagreement between the two reasoners was marked by violent sectional, ideological, and economic conflicts that reverberate to this day.

To put it another way, the theme of reason tells us little about the blood, sweat, and tears of Jefferson's politics or those of his enemies. This is not only a political biography but also, alas, a superficial one. It is a verbal icon, a printed and bound version of the New Deal era monument in Washington which could make Jefferson palatable to 20th century Americans only by doctoring his quotation about slavery. This is not Malone's Jefferson, though it bears a resemblance to a fragment of that portrait. It is not Nock's or Parrington's or Bowers's or Peterson's or that of many others that could be named. It is George Bancroft's Jefferson. Bancroft was a clever New England scribbler of the 19th century who, unable to defeat Jefferson, took a narrow slice of him and created a putative whole that he found compatible. Exactly the same thing happened more recently when George Will and others converted Ronald Reagan, at one time a wild man from the West and potential threat to the Establishment, into just another Republican, tolerable if not beloved in Boston and Hartford.

After the violent twist of American society away from his dispensation in the later 19th century, Jefferson can be made to fit consensus history only by a good deal of selective emphasis. Cunningham thus follows the standard interpretation that Jefferson's allegiance to states' rights was merely a temporary expedient, adopted for the occasion, for the larger goal of the defense of civil liberties. But this is unhistorical. In his own time and several generations later, the Kentucky Resolutions of 1798, affirming state sovereignty, were the core of his political position. (Here we run into the mystification heaped up by the cleverly vengeful industry of several generations of Adamses, who convinced most later observers that Jefferson's presidency was a contradiction of his earlier position. It was not so seen by most at the time or for many decades following.)

The real Jefferson, by modern interpretation, put freedom ahead of states' rights. This is to indulge in a too-easy make-over of Jefferson to please ourselves and to miss the main point, which is that for Jefferson—and his followers—the two were synonymous and inextricable. It is self-evident in the historical record for those who have eyes to see, obvious to anyone who will read Jefferson's correspondence through from the 1790's to the 1820's or who will examine the context—the understanding of what his career meant to his supporters in his own time. And it is only thus that we can resolve what many 20th century commentators have seen as a contradiction in Jefferson—the theoretical advocate of freedom who engaged on other occasions in what an ACLU devotee would regard as acts hostile to civil liberties. But there is no contradiction between the Jefferson who invoked state sovereignty against the federal sedition law and the Jefferson who approved Virginia's summary execution of a Tory marauder. The contradiction is in the eye of the beholder who attributes to Jefferson a set of assumptions which were not his own. From the point of view of state sovereignty, the two positions are perfectly consistent and democratic. In his role as a public man he trusted Virginia, and her sister and daughter states, to exercise power responsibly when necessary without permanent danger to liberty. (He had his doubts about greedy and self-righteous New Englanders and certain other Americans who were too impressed by Old World arrangements of authority or who had too many plots and plans for the use of public power.) Late in life, when he was no longer an active politician, Jefferson explicitly recommended the use of state interposition against unconstitutional internal improvements legislation—not a question of civil liberties and exactly what was forwarded a very few short years later by Calhoun against the tariff.

Nothing could be more wildly irrelevant to Jefferson's position that liberty was best preserved by protecting the free American social fabric from the federal government, with such exercises of power as were unavoidable left to the wisdom of the people of the states—than that of the modern civil libertarian that freedom is something granted by the federal Bill of Rights after being wrested away from an untrustworthy state majority. In fact, Jefferson's view would still work. Could we restore real federalism and limit the central government to war, diplomacy, and a few other necessary common functions, we could come as close as possible in an imperfect world to settling our major social problems. There is, in fact, no other possible solution for abortion, rampant crime, deteriorating education, and many other evils than a reassumption of power close to the people. It is true we would lose Massachusetts and a few other states of the Deep North, as Jefferson always did, but most of the states would govern themselves "reasonably," could they decide without interference. But this will never happen, not because of any defect in the Constitution but because of defects in the national character. It would not in the least have surprised Jefferson that a people who are no longer a nation of independent and public-spirited freeholders but a mass of consumers leavened by an occasional busybody reformer would have difficulty in governing themselves "by reason."

Here we must admit that Jefferson's was a creative and speculative intellect, which bruited a great many ideas in a great many forms to a great many people. Polite and imaginative and fond of discussion, he often adapted himself to his correspondent in a speculative vein, leaving the literal-minded with the impression that he agreed with them. But Jefferson always perfectly understood the difference between theoretical speculation and the real world of American free-holders, and as a public man he was eminently practical and consensus-oriented, as Alexander Hamilton discerned when he refused to countenance the efforts of his fellow Federalists to steal the election of 1800 for the charming scoundrel Burr. Jefferson was, as we said, a complex man. The failure to distinguish between the philosopher and the political leader has led some to regard him as inconsistent or hypocritical and others to take his theoretical projections as literal policy prescriptions. But there is really no problem if one takes care to understand the context of a quotation. Contrary to later assumptions, it was not Jefferson the philosophe who was revered and followed by his contemporaries and a majority of several succeeding generations but Jefferson the sane and balanced public man, not the author of "All Men Are Created Equal" but the republican gentleman who had averted Federalist usurpation. Cunningham presents not this latter Jefferson but rather that partial one who was pleasing to international philosophes and to the more belated and lukewarm of his supporters.

Jefferson's views on slavery, or rather the reaction to them by 20th century intellectuals, or the 20th century public for that matter, provide a fascinating case study in emotional avoidance of simple and obvious historical facts, in the great lengths that people will go to rationalize fantasies that they find comfortable. Cunningham's approach is again the conventional one, to emphasize Jefferson's antislavery sentiments, which, unfortunately, came to little. The whole story is less comforting to those who insist that figures of the past be like them. There is, indeed, a certain childish willfulness in the American mind that insists on chastising persons of other ages for not being like them, or else pretending that they were. Which is a certain way not to learn anything from history.

As to slavery, Jefferson was born into the higher ranks of a social system that long had been, was, and would long continue to be committed to it. He believed, as did many others, and often said, that on balance the situation was deleterious to the commonwealth and it ought to be done away with, if this were possible without damage to other values and interests. His speculations on the nature and relations of the races were deeper, but not much different in conclusions than those of his neighbors and most other Americans of his time.

He was, like his neighbors, committed to keeping the issue in the control of those whose concern it was. His famous letter (to John Holmes) during the Missouri controversy ("We have a wolf by the ears") has been repeatedly misrepresented by those who prefer ideological fantasy to accurate history. What is usually emphasized about the letter is that Jefferson was still committed to his antislavery sentiments, which is true but a misemphasis. In this letter, very clearly (and in many other statements at the same time), Jefferson was not pointing to the evils of slavery, he was pointing to the evils of antislavery, of free-soilism.

The letter is written to console a northerner in trouble with his constituents for favoring the compromise—that is, for favoring the admission of Missouri as a slave state. It is not slavery that Jefferson fears as "the death knell of the Union," it is antislavery, the notion that has been raised for the first time that Congress could tamper with the institutions of new states as a condition for admission. Looked at over the whole career and not sugar-coated and spiffed up to meet 20th century standards, that is to say, viewed historically, Jefferson's views are easily understood and did not differ, except for being more detached in tone (as befitted an elder statesman), from those of most other Southerners of that time and later, including the leaders of the Confederacy. Those views were the exact opposite of, and hostile to, the Free-Soilers of the mid-19th century who claimed him as patron saint. Like all Southerners, Jefferson was unwilling to entertain outside interference.

That we have so nearly lost touch with Jefferson is nowhere better indicated than in his being claimed as the father of modern public education. Jefferson proposed for Virginia a system of public education, never fully implemented, designed not to supplant private education but to supplement it. His main concern beyond making rudimentary learning widely available was to rescue those gifted young men who appeared from time to time in the lower orders of society. He would provide them with the means and the opportunity, in a vigorously competitive and elitist setting, to progress into the aristocracy so that their talents would not be lost to themselves and to society. (The rich would, of course, see to their own success.) Nothing could be further from Jefferson's plan than the programmatic use of the schools as an arm of the state to rearrange society (though he did favor a necessary orthodoxy of political teaching in support of republicanism which our civil libertarians, committed to leftist revolution, will not allow).

Our public school system was built upon a Massachusetts-Prussian model that proceeded from the beginning with nearly opposite goals. Its purpose was to provide not leaders but a docile work force and conformist citizenry. Possibly this goal was even a good one given the conditions of the later 19th century, but it was not Jefferson's. Jefferson, defender of the aristocracy of talents against the aristocracy of privilege, would find anathema a school system which expends vast resources in the hope of making marginal improvements in the minds of the dull-witted, while neglecting, demoralizing, and alienating the talented. (The main function of American public education is to make sure that the talented poor do not get a good education and are not able to rise and compete with the class that can afford private schooling, a class noted for its sterling verbal commitment to egalitarian public education.)

This brief sketch, I believe, captures something of the essential Jefferson. But, of course, history is many things and serves many purposes, and its fascination lies just in the fact that it is not and never can be definitive. Professor Cunningham has enjoyed a pleasant and prestigious appointment, by no means a sinecure, to provide a new account of Jefferson's life in relatively short compass. If one wants a reliable, factual, well-written overview of the life of Jefferson the public man, in some but not too great detail, then this book will serve the purpose. It is a pleasant but not very invigorating diversion for those who like their American history as untroubled as possible. And I have no doubt that a great many more readers will prefer Cunningham's filter tip cigarette to the pungent but authentic plug of old Virginia bright leaf that I have proffered above.

15.

HAMILTON AND JEFFERSON

A review of *How Alexander Hamilton Screwed Up America* by Brion McClanahan

A THINKING AMERICAN must choose between Hamilton and Jefferson, whose contrary visions of the future were contested in the first days of the Constitution. If you are happy with big government, big banks, big business, big military, and judicial dictatorship, then you have Alexander Hamilton to thank. His legacy of nationalism, centralisation, crony capitalism, and military-industrial complex is all around us.

If you prefer the Jeffersonian version of an American regime (or even if you don't), Brion McClanahan's new book is for you— *How Alexander Hamilton Screwed Up America*. McClanahan, who is proving to be one of the ablest truly relevant historians of our time, has given us a definitive, deeply-researched chapter and verse and long perspective of who this bad man was and how he is, Constitutionally, the fountain of our current discontents.

When Hillary Clinton called we Americans "deplorables" (in contrast to the rich foreign sophisticates who surround her) she was simply channeling Alexander Hamilton who said that "the people are a great beast."

Hamilton's final resting place is the old Episcopal church just off Wall Street, one of the few early buildings left in Manhattan. I once visited a friend who was working on Wall Street and was told that the stockbrokers and bankers have a tradition of keeping fresh flowers on Hamilton's grave. Nothing could be more appropriate.

And it is a measure of Hamilton's dominance of the American regime that the habitués of Wall Street are now immensely powerful and respectable. Hamilton's Jeffersonian opponents called them "speculators" and "jobbers." Not that Jeffersonians were opposed to enterprise or honest pursuit of profit. But for them Hamilton's friends were engaged in dubious machinations to prey on the wealth produced by others, plausible extortion using the government and co-opting the rest of society into their schemes. There is certainly enough corruption in the history of Wall Street and the connected banking interests to lend credibility to the Jeffersonian view.

This book is a deeply researched and well thought out examination of how the immigrant bastard (literally) on the make, Hamilton, lied the Constitution into a centralisation and elite wealth-producing instrument that was not the limited federal government ratified by the people of the States. He laid the foundations that subsequent Supreme Court usurpers like John Marshall, Joseph Story, and finally Hugo Black, used to turn the original Constitution upside down.

Remember this—Hamilton and Marshall and Story and their accomplices lied. In office, they clandestinely repudiated their statements made while encouraging ratification of the Constitution and immediately began to reinterpret it by verbal gymnastics and false history. Their goal, successful over time, was to establish the centralised regime that had been repudiated by the American people in the Philadelphia Convention and the ratifying conventions.

The lying centralisers said they were working for a stronger government for a better country. This may have been sincere, but we miss here the hidden engine of motivation for this political movement—greed. The desire for a government to profit those who could manipulate it. Federalists moaned about the danger of democracy. The wild majority might vote themselves the wealth of their betters. A strong "energetic" executive and supreme judiciary were needed to prevent this.

But as John Taylor replied to John Adams, this is not the way it usually happens. Rather, the people go about their business quietly unless greatly provoked. The danger is from interested minorities of the clever and well-connected who have endless devices to use the government to become parasites of the real wealth producers.

For Hamilton, a government debt was "a public blessing," making for a strong and stable government. Meaning that the wealthy could increase their wealth through the tax-free interest on government bonds paid by the duped taxpayers. (Not to mention that the U.S. government with its vast income did not need to borrow money if it stayed with its Constitutional functions.) Then the United States must have "a stable currency." Meaning that the government turned over its power to a cartel of private bankers who had the immense power and profit of controlling the currency. And there must be a high tariff "to protect American labour." Meaning that Northern manufacturers had captive customers and could charge above market prices for their goods. And, of course, the government must be able to act vigorously. Meaning to slap down those deplorables who resisted the taxes imposed by their betters.

We must face the fact that the Constitution has been progressively distorted by falsehoods. Most law professors, "constitutional" scholars, and judges do not have a clue as to the truly federal system the Constitution was supposed to establish. This is true even of most "originalists" like the Federalist Society, for whom "original intent" is found in Marshall's decisions. As McClanahan notes in conclusion, the real and only solution to our present dilemma is a return to the real Constitution and the very limited government that it intended. We must eschew Hamilton and return to the Constitution of Jefferson's Kentucky Resolutions and the immensely wise policy prescriptions of Jefferson's first inaugural address.

The author has in a short span of years published *9 Presidents Who Screwed Up America, The Politically Incorrect Guide to the Constitution, The Politically Incorrect Guide to Real American Heroes,* and other books. This is a remarkable achievement. McClanahan has proved to be one of the most productive and original historians of the current time: a historian in the great tradition, not one of the conformist academic bureaucrats who now pose as the "historical profession."

16.

WHY THEY HATE JEFFERSON

Review of *The Long Affair: Thomas Jefferson, and The French Revolution* by Connor Cruise O'Brien

WHAT A MARATHON OF JEFFERSON-BASHING we have had in the last few years. This book by the "global statesman" O'Brien follows several other critical biographies, all of which have been highlighted in the fashionable reviews. More than usually offensive to Jefferson admirers was a collection (*The View from Monticello*) by University of Virginia professors trashing their founder (not surprising since they are all carpetbaggers anyway); a slashing attack in *National Review*; and, worst of all, Ken Burns's latest television "documentary."

None of this literature tells us anything about Jefferson. There is no scholarship—that is, research and discovery—involved. We have here, rather, a case study in intellectual sociology: that is, an exhibit by fashionable intellectuals determining what is and is not acceptable to their version of the American regime. What they tell us is that Jefferson is out now.

Friends, you must have either Jefferson or Hamilton. All the fundamental conflicts in our history were adumbrated during the first decade of the General Government in the contest symbolized by these two men. Hamilton lost in the short run, but triumphed in the long run. He would find much that is agreeable in the present American regime—a plutocratic kritarchy which we persist, by long habit of self-deception, in calling a democracy. But Thomas Jefferson would not be at all happy with what has happened to this country; he might even suggest that the time had come for a little revolution. The host of petty intellectuals and pundits, elitists, and would-be elitists—tame scribblers of the American Empire— sense this, and so Jefferson must be dealt with appropriately. The Establishment is frightened by the rumblings they hear from the Great Beast (that is, we the American people). They are shocked to realize that Jefferson honestly did believe in the people; that he believed the soundest basis for government to be popular consent and severely limited officials.

Hamilton, on the other hand, believed in rule by "the [self-appointed] best" and in "energetic government" operating in the interest of private profit. For the better part of a century we had protective tariffs which burdened the great mass of the American people, agriculturalists and consumers, while profiting large capital. Now that it is in the interest of large capital to ship American workers' jobs to the Third World, we have every petty pundit singing the praises of "free trade." Just what Alexander ordered.

Hamilton, it is true, was rather indifferent to the do-gooder side of the federal leviathan. Yet do-gooderism was axiomatic for the New Englanders who made up the largest base of his support: people whose instinct is immediately to translate every moral prompting into governmental coercion.

O'Brien's brief against Jefferson is twofold. First, he favored the French Revolution, even its excesses, which show him to be an irresponsible bloody-minded parlor revolutionary. Second, Jefferson was not a racial egalitarian and is therefore an unacceptable symbol for modern America.

O'Brien, as a number of reviewers have pointed out, lacks the most fundamental requirement of historianship—that is, the careful use of documents and understanding of context. He makes no distinction between Jefferson's friendship for the French people—his always cautious hopes that they might achieve popular government—and support for the Terror. On this subject (as on most others), there is much better treatment from Albert Jay Nock's old biography, *Jefferson*. As for Jefferson not being a racial egalitarian—well, neither were Lincoln, Teddy Roosevelt, and Woodrow Wilson or, for that matter, Harry Truman and Ike Eisenhower. So what?

What we have here is elitist hysteria, an old and familiar phenomenon. During the election of 1800, the president of Yale, Timothy Dwight, stumped New England trying, with the aid of most of the New England clerisy, to convince the people that Jefferson was a representative of the Illuminati. John Adams cowered in his fortified house in fear of The Mob, while Jefferson lived at ease among his 200 slaves. The Federalists persuaded themselves that the guillotines were about to be set up if that horrible decadent Southerner were elected, ousting them from their power and prestige. Today, we have merely the latest version of the thing. Petty elitists, unsure of their unmerited positions and fearful of the people, conjure up a dark spectacle of terror. How unthinkable that we should have those yahoos out there calling the shots, instead of their betters.

The trouble is, Jefferson was always a liberal but never a Liberal. Liberals (for lack of a better term) for years perpetuated an elaborate hoax making Jefferson one of them—which he never was or could have been. Now that it is obvious that he really wasn't, an elaborate ex-communication—equally a hoax—from the American canon seems to them necessary. It would be comedic if it were not such a malicious perversion of the historical truth. The burden of O' Brien's teaching is that Jefferson does not belong in, and must be ejected from, the American civil religion. But does America have a civil religion? Ought we to have one? Who says so? And if we do, do we need some damned foreigner to tell us what is to be left in, and what out, of it? What Jefferson most fundamentally signifies is that we do not need secular priests governing our civic life; we need merely to trust in a limited, popular government while keeping a wary eye on the self-appointed clerisy.

The pundits are right. Jefferson does not offer aid and comfort to the present regime. And let us thank the Creator who endowed us with our inalienable rights for that. We still have in Jefferson a powerful symbol for liberty and the consent of the people that no number of pettifogging scribblers can suppress.

A LOST AMERICAN LEGACY

17.

Thomas Jefferson's Birthday

THOMAS JEFFERSON'S BIRTHDAY went virtually unnoticed earlier this year (1993), the 250th anniversary of his birth. Nothing is more indicative of how badly we Americans have squandered our moral capital and betrayed the substance of our history. We did have, of course, President Clinton's inaugural journey from Monticello, though it is hard to imagine anything further from the true spirit of Jeffersonian democracy than the motley crew of socialists, spoilsmen, image manipulators, and foreign agents who make up the present leadership of the Democratic Party (except perhaps the motley crew of stockjobbers, spoilsmen, image manipulators, and foreign agents who make up the leadership of the Republican Party).

Then there was the conference on "Jeffersonian Legacies," held at Mr. Jefferson's University and since issued as a book and a videotape for PBS, that was devoted to a motley lot of dubiously qualified northeastern and California intellectuals preening about how much wiser and more enlightened they are about racial matters than Mr. Jefferson. In fact, Jefferson's discussion of the American racial dilemma in Query XIV of *Notes on the State of Virginia* says everything true that can be said about the subject, ethically and intellectually, as will be seen a hundred years from now, should there be any men and women left who are capable of Jefferson's range, clarity, honesty, and detachment.

Jefferson had the most capacious mind and, until his later years, the most optimistic temperament of any of the Founders. Had he never held a public office, his vast corpus of letters and writings would still be one of our most important legacies from that era. He was, on one side of his personality, a true intellectual, fond of ideas and speculation. The dull-witted and literal-minded have continually taken his statements out of context as dogmatic proposals to be enforced or opposed, failing to distinguish, as he did himself, between Jefferson the American public man and President and Jefferson the international man of letters.

Conservatives, in particular the heirs of his enemies, the Federalists, have had a hard time with Jefferson, often finding in him the anticipation of all they hate. Which is just the reverse of the counterfeit coin peddled by the leftists of the 20th century who once made him an unrecognizable idol (though they thankfully are no longer much inclined to do so). In other words, Jefferson has been erected again and again into a straw man to worship or to execrate. He is bigger than all of the trivial images that have been constructed. To rediscover him we must unravel layer after layer of misrepresentations piled up by successive generations of self-centered interpreters. For instance, on the slavery question, liberal intellectuals made him one of them, and then attacked him for hypocrisy when they discovered that he wasn't. But this is silly. Jefferson was himself, easily discernible all along to any honest observer, and under no obligation to conform himself to the categories of trivial thinkers of later generations.

Conservatives, misled by some of the more unscrupulous opponents of his own time, have had problems with Jefferson's religion. Undoubtedly, he tended toward deism, as did many of the intelligent men of his time to some degree or other. But Jefferson was never an enemy of religion, despite the hysterical charges of New England preachers unhinged by the French Revolution and their personal loss of deference.

Jefferson always conducted his family life within the Anglican communion, in contrast to John Adams, who is invariably described as an upholder of orthodoxy though he became a Unitarian (!) not out of youthful folly but of a mature decision.

Jefferson the public man was in fact the favorite candidate of the more tolerant Protestant denominations and religious minorities. What he opposed was what he called "priestcraft," by which he meant the clergy of New England hell-bent on dominating the minds and actions of other men by force rather than free assent. The "priestcraft" has degenerated from Calvinist to transcendentalist and now to Cultural Marxist, but the impulse remains the same.

Likewise, Jefferson's educational system has been praised and condemned as the progenitor of our modern public school establishment. But the debased system we have comes from Prussia by way of the New England reformers Horace Mann and John Dewey. Its rationale is egalitarian and regimented "progress." The goal of Jefferson's proposed educational system was excellence and the rescue of talent from obscurity for the good of the commonwealth. A resemblance is apparent only to the terminally shallow who mistake words for things.

The process of Jeffersonian obscurantism began early in the 19th century, when the village atheists of New England, from Emerson on down, who execrated Jefferson the public man, began to appropriate selective words of Jefferson the philosophe as ammunition in their own will to power ("priestcraft"). This was their common way of proceeding. For instance, at the same time they managed to turn the fox-hunting cavalier George Washington into a puritan prig congenial to themselves.

The process reached culmination in the 1850's, when a new party stole the name of Jefferson's party, "Republican," to cover a platform of business subsidy, abolitionist agitation, and Puritanism—all things that Jefferson abhorred. It would never have occurred to him that his own personal philosophical position could be employed by very different men as an ideological juggernaut to coerce his fellow citizens by federal force. Jefferson the public man led and reflected a public consensus, not an ideological program. It was very clear to his own generation, and the subsequent generation or two in those parts of the country that followed him, what that consensus was.

Jefferson and his friends came to power (the "Revolution of 1800") in opposition to the economic and moral imperialism of Hamilton and his friends—a program of taxes, manipulation of the economy for the inevitable benefit of the few and the burden of the many, moral dragooning of the population, and involvement in foreign power politics. It was this threat that Jefferson and his friends put down, and kept down, for half a century—the happiest era of the Union.

Jefferson the philosophe is of great intellectual interest but of little political relevance to our very different, chastened age. It is Jefferson the public man we need to recover, as well as his program and his party: adherence to the limits of federal power in the Constitution; preservation of the rights of the states as the chief bulwark of our liberties (the "Principles of 1798," toasted by Jeffersonians for generations); low taxes; a simple and economical government that interferes as little as possible in the activities of the citizens; avoidance of "entangling alliances."

This was the platform of Jefferson the leader who postponed Hamiltonian calamities to the Republic and who was loved by the preponderance of the American people in his own time and long after. It is that Jefferson we need and who is our greatest asset against high-handed elites who oppress the people in the name of equality and popular rule. It is that Jefferson who said: "There is a natural aristocracy among men. The grounds of this are virtue and talent." "I am not among those who fear the people. They, and not the rich, are our dependence for continued freedom. And to preserve their independence, we must not let our rulers load us with perpetual debt. We must make our election between economy and liberty, or profusion and servitude."

Once Jeffersonian democrats were the most numerous of all American political types. During the second half of the 20th century, they have scarcely been heard from. Yet, in my opinion, there are, out there in the hinterlands, millions of us waiting for a reassertion of the "Principles of 1798" and for another "Revolution 1800." But alas, we wait in vain for another Jefferson to lead.

18.

Jeffersonians Against Imperialism

J. William Fulbright, *The Arrogance of Power,*
1966, and *The Price of Empire,* 1967.

Robert C. Byrd, *Losing America: Confronting a*
Reckless and Arrogant Presidency, 2004

KNOWN AND CELEBRATED AS A "LIBERAL" during the
Vietnam War era, Fulbright was actually a quite independent
minded public figure. In some respects, he represented a remnant
of the Southern Democratic Jeffersonian tradition, and he was
never anti-South. It is said that John F. Kennedy wanted Fulbright
for Secretary of State, but declined to nominate him because of
massive criticism of his pro-South views.

James William Fulbright (1905–1995) was a Senator
from Arkansas 1945–1975, losing his 30-year seat because of
opposition to the Vietnam War. Liberals celebrated Fulbright for
that opposition, without realising that while they opposed the
war because it was anti-Communist, he opposed it because of the
dread of the damage done to America by commitment to a military

empire. Fulbright wrote that setting out to police the world and rescue mankind avoided dealing with internal problems and destroyed our hallowed tradition of inspiring by example.

A similar position was taken by another representative of the last Southern Democrat power in national affairs. Robert C. Byrd of West Virginia, Senator 1959–2010, questioned the wisdom of the Vietnam War. He vigorously opposed the U.S. expedition into Iraq, as indicated in his speeches and his 2004 book *Losing America: Confronting a Reckless and Arrogant Presidency.* Alas, by the time Byrd wrote it, anti-war had become a leftwing syndrome and Southern politics had been absorbed by party-first empty suit Republicans.

Southerners have the reputation of supporting U.S. wars. We value honourable self-defense and effective replies to real enemies, and are the first to volunteer to go into harm's way. But we have never thought that war was a noble crusade to spread democracy, which is always the national default excuse for American aggression. I remember with shame how many of us were foolishly led into supporting the Vietnam War. The antiwar movement was so arrogant and unpatriotic that it seemed natural to support the war. We should have thought further. We had become too much American and too little Southern.

There is a substantial tradition of Southern opposition to unwise imperial wars. Randolph of Roanoke spoke against the War of 1812. John C. Calhoun questioned the way that the Mexican War came about. President Polk had brought on war from a border incident so that Congress had little choice but to accept it. This was a terrible precedent, Calhoun accurately predicted. Calhoun sacrificed a good deal of popularity by insisting on limited war aims and warning that American liberty could not survive a plunge into imperial rule of other peoples.

Populists like Tom Watson of Georgia opposed the Spanish-American War, the annexation of Hawaii and other U.S. imperial ventures. President Cleveland sent a Georgia Congressman and former Confederate officer to try to counter the Republican-supported illegal takeover of Hawaii by New England profiteers and pseudo-moralists.

Perhaps the most sterling example of Southern opposition to war is given by Claude Kitchin. Kitchin served in the U.S. House representing the Old Republican Nathaniel Macon's home district in North Carolina. He sacrificed his leadership position in the House by opposing Woodrow Wilson's maneuvers to get America involved in the European bloodbath of World War I. Other anti-war people praised him as the strongest fighter in their cause.

While others celebrated the glory of an aggressive U.S. and its supposed righteous mission in the world, these Southern critics were concerned with the effects on American republicanism and the Constitution of the drive for world power. It was a remnant of Jeffersonian sentiment, a sentiment of people for whom America was a people and not a theory. Despite all the imitative pro-war hoopla by those Southerners who want to be good "Americans," a remnant on the old Jeffersonian tradition survives and may even be ready for a comeback.

19.

A JEFFERSONIAN POLITICAL ECONOMY

*I tremble for my country when I reflect
that God is good.*—Thomas Jefferson

FROM ITS BEGINNINGS, the U.S. government was regarded by Southerners as a matter of liberty, honour, and American mutuality. From its beginnings, the predominant class in the North regarded the government as their money-making machine. Southerners saw the Constitution as the people's control over government power. Northerners saw it as an instrument to be manipulated to their advantage. This difference first came to a head in the struggle between Hamilton and Jefferson. Hamiltonians wanted a strong central government built on patronage to the wealthy. The patronage was to be paid through national debt, manipulation of the currency by a "national bank," and various types of business subsidy, which were falsely claimed to be necessary and beneficial to all Americans and essential for good government.

The Jeffersonian position on the role of the federal government in the economy was succinctly stated by a newspaper in 1843: FREE TRADE, NO DEBT, SEPARATION OF GOVERNMENT AND BANKS. It was taken for granted that this included

143

modest government spending, restricted to the clearly stated Constitutional powers and duties of Congress as spelled out in Article I, section 8.

Jeffersonianism has remained a real and long-lasting tradition of thought. It underlays the formation of American colonial society. There was a reason that an English poet referred to Virginia as "the earthly paradise." Because those who had no hope of independent status at home could there attain it there. This describes the spirit that underlays the American War of Independence and Jeffersonian opposition to Hamiltonianism.

Since 1861 the Jeffersonian political economy has been a very weak force. Every principle that its spokesmen advocated has been crushed and everything they warned against has become only too true.

No philosophy has ever offered a more fundamental criticism of the American system and state capitalism than the Jeffersonian tradition. I deliberately use the term "state capitalism" to describe the regime in which the government does not operate in the interest of free enterprise, which is the comforting myth, but is the agent for protecting and adding to great private wealth. The Jeffersonian critique of capitalism is far more fundamental than the Marxist one. Marxists love and encourage state capitalism because it is a step towards government control of the economy. The Jeffersonian tradition upholds private property and freedom of enterprise against their enemies, socialism and big capitalism—the dominance of government-enhanced wealth over general well-being.

Jeffersonians (including a valiant minority of Northerners) managed to hold Hamilton's schemes within limits for two generations, although they were constantly and aggressively put forward. Lincoln's conquest and near destruction of the South established the Hamiltonian program without any effective check. Yet Jeffersonian ideals continued to wield a certain power long afterward.

The contest between the policies of Hamilton and Jefferson dominated national politics from their time until Lincoln. Each side had victories and defeats until the Republican party took power in 1861, and with the South not voting, implemented Hamiltonian policies with a vengeance—high government expenditure, high tariff, perpetual debt, and a "national" banking system.

Anyone who leaves out the significance of what happened in early 1861, between Lincoln's election and Fort Sumter, and insists it was all about "slavery" will never know the truth about the WBTS. In the first response to secession, Northerners cited the Declaration of Independence on consent of the governed and said "Let the erring sisters go in peace." Abolitionists said they were glad to be free of Southern contamination. Then Congress passed the Republican tariff of almost 50% on most imports. The new Confederate government voted a tariff of 5% and announced that Northerners could have free navigation of the Mississippi river and use of the port of New Orleans. Influential Northerners realized what this would mean. They would lose their captive source of revenue and market in the South. Their profits would nose dive. They might even have to pay taxes themselves. Not only would they lose the South, but it was obvious that the whole Mississippi Valley would prefer to trade through the low tariff Confederacy rather than the United States. In public speeches and private letters, in newspaper editorials and petitions to Congress, and in every other way, influential Northerners let it be known that war was preferable to allowing the South to escape. One could fill several books with such statements. When asked why the South could not be allowed to peaceably secede, Lincoln invariably referred to the loss of revenue—not "slavery."

Until Lincoln, politicians argued about national bank or no national bank, seldom touching the real question, that is, who would control the money supply. In 1863, Senator John Sherman of Ohio, brother of General Sherman, declared that establishing a national banking system was the most important Northern goal of the war. He would leave the slaves as they were rather than lose this system. This is even after the Emancipation Proclamation, and our brilliant historians still tell us that the war was all about slavery.

Their national banking system followed the same plan except that it spread the loot around. The government chartered a series of national banks, endowing them with government bonds at a discount as their capital. These banks could issue money, giving them virtual control of the money supply and credit of the country. Their's was the power to inflate and deflate the currency and to decide what credit there was to be in the economy and at what rate of interest. Obviously, the granting of such charters was political, and open to corruption.

Jeffersonians tried to pay off the national debt and almost succeeded. The U.S. Bank was installed twice and each time allowed to expire after twenty years. When the Republicans got power in 1861, Wall Street urged on the war which would make a national debt. Lincoln and his party were able to install an advanced form of Hamilton's dream that dominates the American economy right up to the present moment.

Lincoln's war created a tremendous debt and the U.S. government continues to borrow money. The government used to finance itself that way when it generally balanced the budget. Now it finances its tremendous deficit spending the same way, debt. The U.S. Congress has long been spending beyond its means year by year, and not because of an emergency, but to buy elections. There is now a debt so tremendous that it can never be paid. To pay it would take all the earnings of you, your children, and your grandchildren to infinity. However, the holders of government bonds do not mind. Merely paying the interest on the debt is now the major part of the budget.

An interesting sidelight that is never mentioned. The Lincoln Republicans, while somewhat emancipating the slaves passed a Contract Labor Law. This allowed companies to collect gangs of workers in Europe, paying their passage over in exchange for being bound to work for a set number of years. Obviously, such workers were very vulnerable, and of course readily available as strike breakers. Some companies had a regular policy of bringing in contract immigrants every certain number of years to keep down wages and union activity. That is why New England can no longer brag that it is pure WASP country. Emancipation anyone? And to think that some people expected the Republicans, the original cheap labour party, to oppose the recent unlawful illegal immigrant amnesty. We might also mention that under Lincolnian legislation the government gave away vast amounts of public lands to railroad and other corporations.

It never occurred to them to give any land to freed African Americans in the South, although they were ready farmers. The role of the black people was to stay in the South, vote for carpetbaggers, and not darken the Northern home front. It is no accident that the Lincoln and Grant administrations are the most corrupt in U.S. history.

The Southern Jeffersonian conception of the good society did not completely disappear even after Lincoln and his party negated it, but long remained in Southern Democratic opposition to Big Business. I might mention the Clayton Antitrust Act of 1914, bearing the name of Representative Henry D. Clayton of Alabama, son of the Confederate general of the same name. And the Glass-Steagall Act of 1932. This law was designed to separate commercial and investment banking and correct some of the abuses that had led to the Great Depression. It carries the names of Senator Carter Glass of Virginia and Representative Henry B. Steagall of Alabama. The repeal of this law by the Reagan administration, according to many experts, caused the crisis of 2007–2008. America was desperately in need of some Jeffersonian insight. The big bankers and brokers had behaved unethically and illegally in an immense scale and the official watchdogs had failed entirely. When the crash came it not only put the Big Fellows in peril of collapse, it also destroyed the wealth of pension funds and small investors.

Note that the only solution to be found by either party was for the taxpayers to "bail out" the misbehaving bankers and brokers so they could continue to draw their multi-million dollar salaries rather than go to jail. The malefactors were judged to be Too Big to Fail and Too Big to Jail. Geither and Paulson, both former officials of Goldman Sachs who had moved into government, were hailed as heroes for finding a way for the taxpayers to bail out the offending banksters. We were told that a multi-billion dollar bailout was necessary to save "our economy." The Economy, Stupid, has become a monstrous god without any interest in the well-being of his people. Now and then his priests inform us what sacrifices We must make to keep in his good graces. We need to remember what prosperity is supposed to feel like. But first we must find out who "we" are.

A Jeffersonian political economy as the ideal was implicit in the Southern classic *I'll Take My Stand*. A few years later, 1936, some of the Twelve Southerners joined some Northern and British writers in a sequel defense of a humane economy—*Who Owns America? A New Declaration of Independence*. The Great Depression had generated much discussion about fundamental reform of the American regime. Communists and socialists were sure they had the answer—government control of property. Progressives thought capitalism could be preserved but the economy could be managed by expert planners like themselves, basically the New Deal approach.

Who Owns America? took a different stand. Who Owns America? Well, might we ask? Both capitalists and socialists, these writers argued, were asking the wrong questions. Both took for granted the gigantic concentration of power over the economy in a few great corporations, only argued over detail. There was little difference between them. Both were for preserving a system in which the mass of people were wage earners at the mercy of owners. This was the wrong kind of society. The U.S. had begun as and for a time had continued to be a society of wide spread property ownership, of independent citizens. Free enterprise and private property are good things. We are all for them, they said. We reject socialism but we also question the existing domination of America by corporate capitalism. As John Taylor of Caroline had pointed out in his great exposition of Jeffersonian political economy, *An Inquiry into the Principles and Policy of the Government of the United States*, a rich country is not the same thing as a happy people. And certainly a rich government is not the same thing as a prosperous people.

As the authors of *Who Owns America?* and *I'll Take My Stand* pointed out, the corporate capitalists in effect own the country and the politicians. What is a corporation? The founding generation considered corporations to be legal monopolies, generally bad things. The Philadelphia convention voted down giving the federal government the right to charter corporations, which did not prevent Alexander Hamilton from insisting on the chartering of a national bank as soon as the government got under way. He said it was "necessary and proper." John Taylor pointed out that this was the first of countless instances where mere verbiage was employed to distort the plain intent of the Constitution.

A corporation is a legal person, except that unlike a person it is immortal and cannot feel pain or guilt. The 14th amendment was supposed to be for giving rights to the newly freed slaves. Shortly after it passed (illegally), the U.S. Supreme Court declared corporations to be legal persons. Like persons, they are said to have rights that may not be interfered with. The Supreme Court thus vetoed numerous efforts of States to regulate the abuses of corporations. Under this cover, corporations proliferated like kudzu and did as they pleased. It can be argued that the unscrupulous Republican sponsors of the 14th amendment intended this all along.

What is corporate property? An individual owns stock in a corporation. What does he own? He owns a right to dividends if there are any. He may sell his stock, for more or less than he paid for it. He is personally liable for the corporation's debts to only a small extent, which is a great advantage to all those participating in the corporation. Unlike a farm or a family business, the corporate stockholder has no practical responsibility for what the corporation does, and most importantly he has no moral responsibility to society, to workers, to turning out a good product. The corporation is in the power of a few men. This is true whether they are business executives, the expert planners of socialism, or the party officials of communism. In each case the happiness of the people is dependent upon remote forces over which they have almost no control. Unlike a society with widespread ownership of productive property, this is not a healthy or a really free society.

The capitalists yell about threats to free enterprise and the evil effects of interference with the law of supply and demand. The trouble is, Big Business never has practiced free enterprise. It is too powerful to tolerate competition. There is a lot of small-scale free enterprise in America, but not in Big Business which controls rather than participates in the free market. The authors pointed out that in the Depression prices of farm products declined by over 30%. But the prices of steel and automobiles did not decline at all. If the law of supply and demand was working, prices should decline with declining demand. Something was interfering with the free market. The large corporations preserved their profits because their foreign competition was excluded by government tariffs and their gigantism guaranteed their ability to stifle any potential domestic competition. The only real solution offered by the New Deal was to flood the economy with cheap money so as to increase demand, which might help unemployment but would also keep profits up. So much for free enterprise.

Further, giant corporations did not exist because concentration is economic law. Industry was not controlled by entrepreneurs or managers—it was controlled by bankers. Wealth had come to consist of entries on bankers' books. Such property is infinitely manipulable for private profit. John D. Rockefeller had never done a productive day's work in his life, but he controlled Standard Oil which controlled a large part of the market in the U.S. It was not socialists who hated the fabulously rich Rockefeller, who exhibited his Yankee charity by handing out dimes to Sunday school children. It was entrepreneurs who hated Rockefeller, the men who used their knowledge and risked their money to get the oil out of the ground. They found that Rockefeller capital had bribed state legislatures, rigged railroad rates, bought refineries, and acquired and suppressed new patents that would have cheapened production for small producers. The real producers of wealth were not able to sell their product except on Rockefeller's terms, which usually meant turning over control. I guarantee you that today, when Lawrence Rockefeller of the Chase Manhattan Bank (or whatever they call it now) calls, the President of the United States answers it as soon as he can. The power of the banks is almost never questioned in American public discussion. Now that is real power, when you can prevent yourself from even being mentioned.

And, the authors of *Who Owns America?*, as did those of *I'll Take My Stand*, asked: what is so great about concentration of industry into a few gigantic firms? Is a huge factory necessarily more efficient than many small factories spread through the countryside? It is certainly less humane and makes the workers even more insecure. No, we had giant corporations not because they are efficient but because that is what the bankers want. It makes their control easier and firmer. The bankers always get what they want. We do not want to do away with private property, the authors of this last gasp of Jeffersonian political economy said— we want to see policies that will spread it around, that will curb the corporations and increase the number of people who have enough property to make an independent living. Of course, the program of *Who Owns America?* was too humane, too lacking in money to buy politicians and media, too unappealing to the vast herd of petty intellectuals who dominate American discourse. It could not succeed, and America has paid the price.

For Jeffersonians, economic health is not measured by the day's average of stock speculation, or the profits of bankers, or the munificence of government subsidies and salaries, or the consumption of luxury goods, or even by the Gross Domestic Product. Economic health is when the great bulk of families have some property and a secure source of living, large or small. When nearly everybody has an abundance of necessities and access to some small luxuries and leisure. Naturally, debt, the ancient nemesis of prosperity, is minimal and temporary in a prosperous society. For both government and people it is a device for emergencies or starting up promising ventures. A healthy society is made up mostly of people of middling economic status, with relatively few very rich and very poor. Government apparatus is small, unobtrusive, and mainly local. Religion, charity, education, and the arts flourish, especially where there is cultural cohesion. Cultural cohesion would seem to be typical of societies with widely shared prosperity. The U.S. is catastrophically short of cultural cohesion today.

Declining general prosperity and vast, ever-increasing inequality in wealth are now settled facts of American life. A tiny minority of the rich have reached levels of wealth unprecedented in human history, and are internationalists rather than Americans, happy to ship abroad the livings of their fellow countrymen or import hordes of aliens to replace them.

The triumph of Hamilton and Lincoln has not been a good thing. The consequences of this loss of social morale could in the long run be more serious than a revolution or world war. Many observers have noted with alarm that American society is taking on characteristics of the third world—a few fabulously rich and an immense population of poor.

20.

Some Jeffersonian Wisdom

"The banks are a greater threat to our liberty than standing armies."
—Thomas Jefferson

"...neither the representatives of a nation, nor the whole nation itself assembled, can validly engage debts beyond what they can pay in their own time."

—Thomas Jefferson to Madison on public debt
"at the threshold of our new government."

"...and banknotes will become as plentiful as oak leaves."
—Thomas Jefferson

"They [the people], and not the rich are our dependence for continued freedom. And to preserve their independence, we must not let our rulers load us with perpetual debt. We must make our election between economy and liberty, or profusion and servitude. If we run into such debts, as that we must be taxed in our meat and drink, in our necessaries and our comforts, in our labours and our amusements...our people...must come to labour sixteen hours in the twenty-four, give the earnings of fifteen of these to the government..."
—Thomas Jefferson

"A power in government of any form, to deal out wealth and poverty by law, overturns liberty universally, because it is a power by which a nation is infallibly corrupted."

—John Taylor of Caroline

"But an opinion that it is possible for the present generation to seize and use the property of future generations has produced to both parties concerned, effects of the same complexion with the usual fruits of national error. The present age is cajoled to tax and enslave itself, by the error of believing that it taxes and enslaves future ages to enrich itself."

—John Taylor of Caroline

"A crocodile has been worshipped, and its priesthood have asserted that morality required the people to suffer themselves to be eaten by the crocodile."

—John Taylor of Caroline

"We are now making an experiment, which has never yet succeeded in any region or quarter of the earth, at any time, from the deluge to this day. With regard to the antediluvian times, history is not very full; but there is no proof that it has ever succeeded, even before the flood."

—John Randolph of Roanoke

"I said that this Government, if put to the test—a test that it is by no means calculated to endure—as a government for the management of the internal concerns of this country, is one of the worst that can be conceived..."

—John Randolph of Roanoke

"Why should the government pay the expenses of one class of men rather than another?"

—John C. Calhoun

"A habit of profusion and extravagance has grown up utterly inconsistent with republican simplicity and virtue, and which was rapidly sapping the foundation of our government."
— John C. Calhoun

"It was impossible to force the minds of the public officers to the importance of attendance to the public money, because we had too much of it."
— John C. Calhoun

"It has been justly stated by a British writer that the power to make a small piece of paper, not worth one cent, by the inscribing of a few names, to be worth a thousand dollars, was a power too high to be trusted to the hands of mortal man."
— John C. Calhoun

"The banks have ceased to be mere moneyed incorporations. They have become great political institutions, with vast influence over the welfare of the community..."
— John C. Calhoun. 1837

"We must curb the Banking system, or it will certainly ruin the country."
— John C. Calhoun

"Congress shall appropriate no money from the Treasury, unless it be asked and estimated for by the President or some one of the heads of departments...."
— Confederate Constitution

"Every law or resolution having the force of law, shall relate to but one subject, and that shall be expressed in the title."
— Confederate Constitution

"...any judicial or other federal officer, resident and acting solely within the limits of any State, may be impeached by a vote of two-thirds of both branches of the legislature thereof."
—Confederate Constitution

"The President may approve any appropriation and disapprove any other appropriation in the same bill."
—Confederate Constitution

"...no bounties shall be granted from the Treasury...to promote or foster any branch of industry."
—Confederate Constitution

"The consolidation of the States into one vast empire, sure to be aggressive abroad and despotic at home, will be the certain precursor of ruin which has overwhelmed all that preceded it."
—Robert E. Lee, 1866

"Special Privilege, corporate greed, concentrated wealth are divided throughout our Union between those who call themselves Republicans and those who call themselves Democrats, but the difference in name will not forever succeed in hiding from the people the fact that the Democrats of that sort want exactly the same government favors which are demanded by Republicans of that sort.... Through cunningly devised tax systems, bond systems, currency systems, bank systems.... these modern Highwaymen get boundless booty with minimum risk.... Under the Banking and Bonded Systems, all the Roads of Produce lead to the Rome of Imperial Plutocracy.... A fight over the offices there may be, and will be; but never a fight over principles."
—Thomas E. Watson, Southern Populist, 1916

"The present corporate economy cannot do other than oppose the private economy; it must by its very nature continue to lessen private opportunity and the security of the individual; and it must very often and finally propose the corporate exploitation of every individual and private right."

—Richard B. Ransom, Southern Agrarian

"The essence of finance/capitalism is not free trade but free money."

—Richard B. Ransom, Southern Agrarian

"The government is the executive committee of great wealth."
—Frank L. Owsley, Southern Agrarian, 1936

"So not only those who said the words, but the ones who merely heard them, knew what they meant. Which was this: Life and Liberty in which to pursue happiness…And both of them knew what they meant by 'pursue.' They did not mean just to chase happiness, but to work for it….And they both knew what they meant by 'happiness' too: not just pleasure, idleness, but peace, dignity, independence, and self-respect…."

—William Faulkner

"I do not see the national flag flying from the staff of the sycamore, or any decree of the government written on the leaves of the walnut."

—Wendell Berry

"The revolution I believe is now irreversible. Eventually something will happen to shake the foundations. In the meantime, we must do what we can to mitigate it, but our main task is to find our people and leave a record of the permanent things embodied in our tradition."

—Donald Livingston

ABOUT THE AUTHOR

DR. CLYDE WILSON is Emeritus Distinguished Professor of History of the University of South Carolina, where he served from 1971 to 2006. He holds a Ph.D. from the University of North Carolina at Chapel Hill. He recently completed editing of a 28-volume edition of *The Papers of John C. Calhoun* which has received high praise for quality. He is author or editor of more than 20 other books and over 700 articles, essays, and reviews in a variety of books and journals, and has lectured all over the U.S. and in Europe, many of his lectures having been recorded online and on CDs and DVDs. Dr. Wilson directed 17 doctoral dissertations, a number of which have been published. Books written or edited include *Why the South Will Survive, Carolina Cavalier: The Life and Mind of James Johnston Pettigrew, The Essential Calhoun*, three volumes of *The Dictionary of Literary Biography on* American Historians, *From Union to Empire: Essays in the Jeffersonian Tradition, Defending Dixie: Essays in Southern History and Culture, Chronicles of the South, Calhoun: A Statesman for the 21st Century, The Yankee Problem,* and *Looking For Mr. Jefferson.* Dr. Wilson is founding director of the Society of Independent Southern Historians; former president of the St. George Tucker Society for Southern Studies; recipient of the Bostick Prize for Contributions to South Carolina Letters, the first annual John Randolph Society Lifetime Achievement Award, and of the Robert E. Lee Medal of the Sons of Confederate Veterans. He is M.E. Bradford Distinguished Professor of the Abbeville Institute; Contributing Editor of *Chronicles: A Magazine of American Culture*; founding dean of the Stephen D. Lee Institute, educational arm of the Sons of Confederate Veterans; and co-founder of Shotwell Publishing.

Dr. Wilson has two grown daughters, an excellent son-in-law, and two outstanding grandsons. He lives in the Dutch Fork of South Carolina, not far from the Santee Swamp where Francis Marion and his men rested between raids on the first invader.

Published reviews of Clyde N. Wilson's Works

"...great ability in the field of intellectual history ..."
   —*American Historical Review*

"Wilson is, in short, an exemplary historian...who displays formidable talent."
   —Eugene Genovese

" ...masterful interpretation..."
   —*North Carolina Historical Review*

"Here we find magisterial intellectual history...clearly one of the best of his generation of historians."
   —M.E Bradford

"The compelling quality of these essays speaks broadly to the most vital issues of our national history and identity."
   —J.O. Tate, *Chronicles*

"Well-researched, flawlessly accurate, deeply thought-out, well-written, and timely...."
   —James E. Kibler

"—lucid prose and sharp analysis...."
   —*Blue & Gray Magazine*

"...a mind as precise and expansive as an encyclopedia ....the same old preoccupations given new life and meaning by a real mind ...."
   —Thomas H. Landess

"Wilson is brilliant as always and independent of the pc reductionist history of today."
   —Reader Review

"The one good thing about books by Clyde Wilson: You KNOW they are highly credible sources."
    —Reader Review

"Wilson is a great guide to this literature. Reading this is like going to a bookstore with a wonderfully informed, witty old friend."
    —Reader Review

"Clyde Wilson's essays ...place him on the same level with all the unreconstructed greats in modern Southern letters ..."
    —Joseph Scotchie

"Clyde Wilson exhibits the rarest kind of courage—intellectual courage."
    —Columbia *State*

Latest Releases & Best Sellers

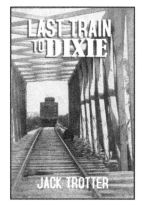

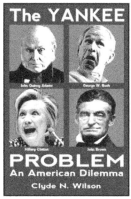

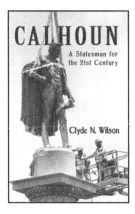

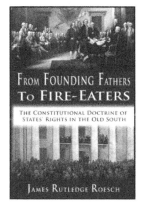

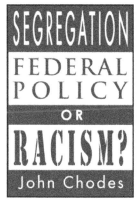

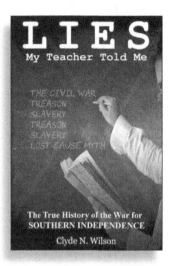

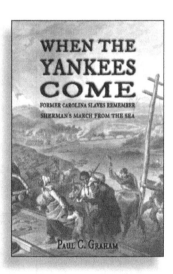

Made in United States
Orlando, FL
17 November 2023

39118657R00098